BP

R

D1323746

Thomson Round Hall Nutshells

Family Law

Is i

ww

Mu

5C

Cl

UNITED KINGDOM

Sweet & Maxwell Ltd
London

AUSTRALIA

Law Book Co. Ltd
Sydney

CANADA AND THE USA

Carswell
Toronto

HONG KONG

Sweet and Maxwell
Asia

NEW ZEALAND

Brookers
Wellington

SINGAPORE AND MALAYSIA

Sweet and Maxwell
Singapore and Kuala Lumpur

Thomson Round Hall Nutshells

Family Law

Louise Crowley
B.C.L., LL.M.

SERIES EDITOR
Bruce Carolan

DUBLIN
THOMSON ROUND HALL
2008

Published in 2008 by
Thomson Round Hall Ltd
43 Fitzwilliam Place
Dublin 2
Ireland

Typeset by Carrigboy Typesetting Services

Printed by ColourBooks, Dublin

ISBN 978–1–85800–500–3

A catalogue record for this book
is available from the British Library.

*The Author and Publisher of this book accept no responsibility whatsoever
for any loss, damage or liability, direct or indirect including consequential
loss, arising from any errors contained herein. Readers are advised that
this book should not be treated as a substitute for legal consultation.*

*All rights reserved. No part of this publication may be reproduced or
transmitted in any form or by any means, including photocopying and
recording, or stored in any retrieval system of any nature without the prior
written permission of the publisher. Application for permission for other
use of copyright material including permission to reproduce extracts
in other published works shall be made to the publishers. Full
acknowledgment of author, publisher and source must be given.*

© Thomson Round Hall, 2008

TABLE OF CONTENTS

TABLE OF CASES

IRELAND

ENGLAND AND WALES

TABLE OF LEGISLATION

CONSTITUTIONAL PROVISIONS

IRISH STATUTES

IRISH STATUTORY INSTRUMENTS

IRISH BILLS

EUROPEAN LEGISLATION

INTERNATIONAL LEGISLATION

1. THE FAMILY AND MARRIAGE

(1) Family law

Introduction

Family law is a unique dichotomy of public and private law, recognising the autonomy of the family unit and its individual members but yet still existing within the confines of state regulation. In truth family law is a mix of both, with the state encouraging and approving private ordering whilst always retaining the right to protect the vulnerable members of the family and of society generally. For example, marriage is a contract between two parties, and it is for the individuals to decide the form their relationship will take and the responsibilities accorded to each of the parties. However, notwithstanding this autonomous right to agree individual obligations and roles, the state has the power to intervene regarding the status of the relationship, the protection of the vulnerable members and it can ultimately dictate financial and property disputes between the parties, which outside the context of the family might otherwise be regarded as an unconstitutional interference with the property rights of one or both of the spouses. Perhaps more importantly the state is empowered to intervene in custody disputes regarding children of the parties and can limit and even deprive one or other of the spouses from contact with the children of the union. This right to intervene is premised on the need to protect the individual members of the family, notwithstanding the elevated status accorded to the family under Irish law and the importance of the family, particularly the marital family in Irish society generally, as discussed below.

Sources of law

Irish family law is derived from numerous sources, including a number of more recently developed sources. The Constitution makes specific reference to the family and its superior position in Irish society. Given the importance of the Constitution as a source of law in the Irish legal system, all other legal enactments and sources must take cognisance of this and cannot conflict with the express special status of the family, limited by the courts to the family based on marriage. Undoubtedly the Constitution has and continues to greatly influence the development and interpretation of all other sources of Irish family law.

1

Influence of the Catholic Church teachings on Irish family law

Historically, the Church has had a major influence on Irish family law, and influenced very significantly any legislative or judicial developments in the area. For many years Catholic Church's involvement in the State's approach to the legal regulation of personal choice was not only prevalent, but expected by the people and lawmakers of Ireland. Burley and Regan refer to the manner in which the new Constitution "gave a special place to the moral leadership of the Catholic Church in the Irish state" (Burley J. and Regan F., "Divorce in Ireland: the Fear the Floodgates and the Reality" [2002] 16 I.J.L.P. & F. 202.) They regard the influence of Catholicism as being particularly reflected in Art.41's limitation of the family to one based on marriage, and the identification of the woman's role within the family as one preferably restricted to the domestic duties of a mother and a wife. They further note that it was not until the enactment of legislation from the late 1950s onwards that rights to property, succession and guardianship of children were recognised. In 1950/51 the collapse of the proposed Mother and Child scheme, intended to provide financial and medical support for mothers and children irrespective of the mother's marital or personal circumstances, came about directly as a result of strenuous objections from the Bishops of Ireland, and served as a reminder of the extent of the Church's influence on state policy. This influence was difficult to defeat given the almost absolute affiliation to Catholicism amongst Irish citizens, and perhaps even more importantly, the manner and extent to which the Articles of the Irish Constitution are premised upon the ultimate authority of the Holy Trinity. The Preamble to the Constitution commences as follows: "In the Name of the Most Holy Trinity, from whom is all authority and to Whom, as our final end, all actions both of men and States must be referred ..."

Such deference to the Catholic Church influenced in particular the State's capacity to regulate the family even though it was regarded as autonomous and "superior to all positive law". In more recent years the influence of the Catholic Church has waned and Catholic teachings in respect of the family and personal autonomy are far less relevant to individual and state decisions regarding the regulation of the family and the acceptability of legal remedies for marital breakdown. Kennedy notes the undeniable changes in "social and economic conditions, and [how the] ... accompanying changes in values and policies have raised fundamental questions about the nature, role and limits of the family." (Kennedy F., "Family, Economy and Government in Ireland" ESRI General Research Series Paper No. 143, January 1989, at 9.)

Comprehensive legislative regulation of the family begins

After many years of an approach of minimal intervention, the Irish legislature has been remarkably active in the area of family law since 1964, but particularly since 1976 which saw the enactment of a series of Acts designed to introduce dedicated legislation in relation to spousal and child maintenance (Family Law (Maintenance of Spouses and Children) Act 1976), domestic violence remedies for spouses and children (Family Law (Protection of Spouses and Children) Act 1976) and the protection from sale of the family home without the consent of the non-owning spouse (Family Home Protection Act 1976). For the first time, the legislature displayed a willingness to intervene in the autonomy of the marital family and empowered either spouse to seek orders from the court for financial or other relief. Whilst both the courts and the legislature had been willing to and, by virtue of the Guardianship of Infants Act 1964 ("the 1964 Act") was capable of making orders in respect of children, these legislative enactments undoubtedly represented a departure by the lawmakers from their previous non-interventionist approach. The legislature has remained active in the area of family law since this time and has regulated all aspects of familial relationships, including legislation regarding children's rights (Children Act 1997 and Children Act 2001), the regulation of the marital (Domicile and Recognition of Foreign Divorces Act 1986, Judicial Separation and Family Law Reform Act 1989, Family Law Act 1995 ("the 1995 Act"), Family Law (Divorce) Act 1996 ("the Divorce Act"), Family Law (Miscellaneous Provisions) Act 1997) and the non-marital family (Family Law Act 1981, Status of Children Act 1987); both generally and upon the breakdown of the relationship, adoption (Adoption Acts 1952–1998), child abduction (Child Abduction and Enforcement of Custody Orders Act 1991), state inter-vention and provision of care (Child Care Act 1991, Children Act 2001 and Child Care (Amendment) Act 2007), domestic violence (Domestic Violence Act 1996, Domestic Violence (Amendment) Act 2002), and more recently has dealt with the issues arising in relation to the recognition and enforcement of international family law orders (Brussels II Regulation and Brussels II bis Council Regulation 2201/03).

Common law

The common law has developed its body of family law on a very ad hoc, case-driven basis which historically gave rise to a lack of a coherent family law policy. Although no longer the primary or most important source of family law generally in Ireland, the continuing significance and impact of the common law in family law is evident from the ongoing extended discretionary decision-making powers accorded to the judiciary in the context of family law disputes. Despite significant legislative developments in almost all aspects of family law, there almost always exists a judicial discretion to apply those provisions in the circumstances of a particular case and in so doing to develop a jurisprudence which informs later decisions. Many examples of this discretionary-based legislative approach exist; for example, in child custody disputes the courts are obliged to make whatever orders are in the best interest of the welfare of the child (Guardianship of Infant Act 1964, s.3). Whilst the legislature has defined what the concept of welfare is comprised of, significant judicial discretion remains and it is for the court to determine the relevance of each aspect in the circumstances of each case and to decide how the welfare of each child is best met. The decisions will in turn be binding on other judges dealing with similar facts. Similarly under s.20(5) of the Divorce Act the court cannot make any order(s) for ancillary relief unless it would be in the interests of justice to do so. Thus despite the existence of significant and detailed legislative enactments, which set out the factors to be taken into account in making financial relief orders, the courts are given wide and discretionary powers to consider the interests of justice and to decide how they might best be met in a particular case. Thus the common law continues to operate as an important and flexible source of Irish family law.

International influences on Irish family law

Traditionally the family law principles and policies of Ireland and other states were domestically driven and attempts to harmonise laws evident in areas such as commercial law were noticeably absent in this context. The main exception to this was in the area of child abduction, which was necessitated by the international aspect to many such abductions. However in more recent times, the growing recognition of the importance of human rights as a key underlying aspect of the protection of family members has seen the incorporation of the European Convention of Human Rights into the domestic provisions of many individual states. In addition the EU has focused some attention on the family laws of its member states, including Ireland (European Convention on Human Rights Act 2003), giving rise to the various Brussels Conventions which have harmonised aspects of European family law and facilitated cross-border applications and enforcement of orders. Whilst this development is more about establishing jurisdiction and facilitating applications and more effectively ensuring enforcement, it has caused member states to examine the family law policies of other member states, given the relative ease with which individuals can make applications in jurisdictions other than their state of origin.

(2) Family law in practice

Jurisdiction of the Irish courts

Jurisdiction in family law matters is divided across the Irish courts, depending on the nature of the proceedings being issued. For example, up until the enactment of the Family Law Act 1995, only the High Court had jurisdiction in relation to nullity proceedings. Equally in relation to maintenance applications, a monetary limit is placed on the amount of maintenance payable at each court level. Most divorce proceedings are issued in the Circuit Court and the Circuit Court's jurisdiction is unlimited but the High Court also has jurisdiction in relation to divorce proceedings, applicable generally to cases involving couples of high net worth and/or complex legal issues.

Court hearings

Even though Art.34.1 of the Constitution requires that all cases should be heard in public, family law cases have been deemed by the legislature to come within the "special and limited cases" exception requiring a private, *in camera* hearing. In relation to child care proceedings, s.29(1) of the Child Care Act 1991 ("the 1991 Act") provides that virtually all proceedings concerning children will be heard otherwise than in public. Such proceedings are required to be as informal as possible, to the extent that is consistent with the requirements of natural justice. In this regard, the rules of evidence continue to apply, as does the right of examination and cross-examination. However, the judges and legal personnel are not permitted to wear wigs and gowns in these proceedings (Child Care Act 1991, s.29(2) incorporating the provisions of ss.33 and 45 of the Judicial Separation and Family Law Reform Act 1989 ("the 1989 Act")). It is also possible under s.30 of the 1991 Act for the court to proceed in the absence of the child to which the proceedings relate. The court may do so either on its own initiative or on the request of a party to the proceedings but only where it is satisfied that this is necessary for the proper disposal of the case. In separation and divorce proceedings all applications are heard *in camera* unless the court directs otherwise. Again there is a degree of informality to the hearing with neither judges nor counsel wearing gowns or wigs (s.32 of the 1989 Act). In relation to domestic violence proceedings the operation of the *in camera* rule received the attention of the Irish courts recently where it considered the English decision of *McKenzie v McKenzie* [1970] 3 All E.R. 1034 which had allowed the presence of a friend of the applicant in divorce proceedings where he did not have the benefit of legal assistance. In *RD v District Judge Oliver McGuinness and by order of the court BD (notice party)* [1999] 1 I.L.R.M. 549 the High Court considered the application of the husband, who sought to bring an unqualified friend to take notes and quietly assist him in responding to domestic violence proceedings. Following consideration on judicial review, it was determined that such "friend" should only be permitted to attend a hearing where there was overwhelming evidence that a fair hearing could not be secured in the absence of such a person.

(3) The Family under Irish law

The Irish Constitution, as enacted in 1937, emphasised the immensely important function of the family, and specifically the marital family in Irish society. Article 41 declares the family to be "the natural primary and fundamental unit group of Society ... a moral institution possessing inalienable and imprescriptible rights, antecedent and superior to all positive law." Consequently the State guarantees in Art.41.2 to "protect the Family in its Constitution and authority, as the necessary basis of social order and as indispensable to the welfare of the Nation and the State." This special and very elevated status deliberately accorded to the family by the drafters, and the positioning of the family effectively above the remit of lawmakers, reflects the view that the family is undoubtedly the most important Irish social construct. Whilst the Constitution does not expressly define the family, Art.41.3 outlines the State's pledge "to guard with special care the institution of Marriage, on which the Family is founded, and to protect it against attack." By virtue of the inclusion of the Art.41.3 pledge in respect of the marital family, the courts have confined the concept of the family and the application of special protection to the family based on marriage.

The case law surrounding the impact of Art.41 has centred on two primary issues—constitutionally founded personal rights particular to the marital family, and secondly, the obligations of the state towards that family unit. One of the most significant cases to single out the marital family as one that attracts constitutional protection is *McGee v Ireland*

[1974] I.R. 284 which concerned the importation of contraceptives by the applicant, a married woman with four children, such act constituting a criminal offence under Irish law. The Supreme Court held that there exists an unenumerated constitutional right to marital privacy and that inter-spousal family planning decisions were not an appropriate matter to attract state intervention and regulation. However, such a right to privacy was strictly limited to persons who were party to a marriage. Similarly in *Murphy v The Attorney General* [1982] I.R. 241 the court declared aspects of the Income Tax Act 1967 to represent an unconstitutional attack on the married family in circumstances where the earnings of a married couple were more heavily taxed than an equivalent unmarried couple. In confirming the decision of the High Court, Hamilton J. stated that "… in the opinion of the Court [the relevant sections are in] breach of the pledge by the State … to guard with special care the institution of marriage and to protect it from attack." This unique protection of the marital family was further evidenced in the judgment of Walsh J. in *State (Nicholau) v An Bord Uchtála and the AG* [1966] I.R. 567, which confirmed that the rights and duties of the family did not extend to the non-marital family:

> "While it is quite true that un-married persons co-habiting together and the children of their union may often be referred to as a family and have many, if not all, of the outward appearances of a family, and may indeed for the purposes of a particular law be regarded as such, nevertheless so far as Article 41 is concerned the guarantees therein contained are confined to families based on marriage." (643–644)

This narrow interpretation of "the family" continues: the court in *WO'R v EH and An Bord Uchtála* [1996] 2 I.R. 248 more recently confirmed that the de facto family, in this case unmarried parents of a child, is not recognised as deserving of protection under the Constitution and Art.41 can only be invoked by a member or members of a marital family. This distinctive constitutional recognition and protection of the marital family, as created and compounded by judicial pronouncements, has greatly influenced state policy as regards maintaining and supporting the marital union and historically acted as an almost insurmountable obstacle to the introduction of the remedy of divorce. The constitutional preferential treatment of the marital family in Art.41 is twinned with a patriarchal view of the domestic role of the mother within that family unit, with express recognition by the State in Art.41.2.1 "… that by her life within the home, woman gives to the State a support without which the common good could not be achieved." Thus a very particular and protective view of the family based on a marital union with designated gender specific roles, was expressly identified by the 1937 Constitution and has formed the basis for the State's approach to the regulation and resolute defence of the marital family.

Interestingly, despite this quite deliberate constitutional preference for the marital family, the extent to which Art.41 places positive obligations on the state to identify rights or entitlements for the family is open to question. In protecting the family as a collective unit the individual members of that family are not especially protected. In particular, the vulnerable position of the child within the family unit has given rise to a debate on the need for constitutional recognition of the rights of the child. It is evident from recent cases, including *Re Baby Ann,* unreported, Supreme Court, Murray C.J., McGuinness, Hardiman, Geoghegan, Fennelly JJ., November 13, 2006, that the rights of the child are presumed, by virtue of the elevated position of the marital family, to always be best served within that family unit. Certainly the Constitutional preference for a woman to work in the home for the benefit of her family and society generally is not supported by any associated direct financial support. In fact the current income tax regime has eliminated the spousal right to utilise un-used taxation credits of a non-earning spouse. Notwithstanding the content of Art.41.2.1 and the Supreme Court confirmation of the decision in *Murphy v The Attorney General* [1982] I.R. 241, the executive and subsequently the legislature has reduced the net income of spouses where one party chooses to work within the home. Such an approach undoubtedly reflects a prioritisation of market and labour demands over the decisions and needs of this "fundamental unit group in society".

Codification of the legal formalities for marriage

The introduction of the Family Law Act 1995 ("the 1995 Act") finally brought about the codification of the Irish law relating to a valid marriage. Prior to this, marriage law in Ireland was governed primarily by the Church and the formalities to be observed for a valid ceremony were determined by the canon law. In relation to Roman Catholic marriages the canon law continued to govern the formalities required, however the enactment of the Marriages (Ireland) Act 1844 as amended by the Registration of Marriages (Ireland) Act 1863 prescribed the statutory formalities applicable to the solemnisation of marriages other than Roman Catholic. Lord Penzance in *Hyde v Hyde* (1866) L.R. 1 P&D 130 declared that a valid marriage comprised of four key aspects; a voluntary union, for life, of one man and one woman, to the exclusion of all others. This is generally regarded as the traditional common law definition of marriage. The enactment of the 1995 Act finally gave rise to the harmonisation and codification of the requirements in all marriages solemnised in the State. Sections 31–33 of the 1995 Act in particular deal with the formalities required by law for a marriage ceremony to be validly recognised. Section 31 provides that to marry a person must be aged 18 years or over, unless an exemption from this provision is granted by either the Circuit Court or the High Court. Section 33(2) of the Act deals with the right to make an application for an exemption from the three-month notice requirement, such exemption can only be granted if "… it is justified by serious reasons and is in the interests of the parties to the intended marriage". To marry under the age of 18, without this exemption, gives rise to a marriage that is null and void ab initio. Section 32 introduced a new civil notice requirement. All persons intending to marry within the State since August 1, 1996 are required to give at least three months' notice in writing of the intention to marry to the appropriate Registrar. A failure to comply with this requirement will also cause the marriage to be null and void ab initio. Section 3(1) of the Family Law (Miscellaneous) Act 1997 ensures that a marriage will not be invalid by reason only of such notification being made to the incorrect registrar.

Recent reform of marriage formalities laws

The provisions relating to the marriage ceremony, contained in the Civil Registration Act 2004 commenced to have effect from November 2007 and replaced the existing legislation governing the formalities of marriage. The main changes resulting from this were as follows:

- The requirement for three months' notification of intention to marry must be given in person to a Registrar, rather than by post; postal notifications will be permitted only in very restricted circumstances, as prescribed by the Minister.
- All couples giving notification must sign declarations of no impediment and obtain a Marriage Registration Form from a Registrar in advance of the ceremony.
- A Register of Solemnisers of Marriage is to be created and maintained by the General Register Office which will contain a record of all those solemnising a civil or religious marriage.

- Civil marriages can be held at venues other than Registry Offices, provided the venue has been inspected and approved by the HSE in advance of the marriage ceremony. Such a ceremony will require a Registrar to be in attendance to solemnise a marriage at such a venue.
- The residency requirements for civil marriages are removed.

Non-observance or absence of formalities

The general principle outside these requirements is that the non-observance of or a defect in any of the other prescribed formalities for marriage does not invalidate a marriage unless both parties were aware of it at the time of the ceremony. The High Court case of *I.E. v W.E.* [1985] I.L.R.M. 691 concerned non-compliance with s.49 of the Marriages (Ireland) Act 1844 which dealt with the celebration of a marriage in a building not authorised for that purpose. Murphy J. was of the view that to invalidate a marriage for non-compliance with s.49, it was necessary to establish not only that there should have been a conscious disregard of the provisions of the section but that both parties to the apparent marriage should have been aware of the defect. The effect of s.49 is not merely directory, if it is knowingly breached it has the effect of invalidating the marriage. However it was ultimately held that the respondent wife had not been aware of the defects in question at the time of the marriage and thus the marriage was valid.

2. LAW OF NULLITY

Introduction

Marriage has long been defined as a legal union between a man and a woman, that is intended to last for their lifetime. The effect of a decree of annulment is that the marriage is void and never existed in law. The law governing nullity law in Ireland historically vested in the Ecclesiastical Courts, but jurisdiction in respect of suits for nullity of marriage was transferred to the Irish High Court following the enactment of the Matrimonial Causes and Marriage Law (Ireland) Amendment Act 1870. Interestingly the grounds upon which a decree of annulment can be sought are not statutorily stated, all such developments since 1870 have been made by the courts, placing added significance on the judicial pronouncements in this area. The jurisdiction to deal with an application for a decree of nullity was considered by the legislature in the context of the 1995 Act which accorded concurrent jurisdiction in nullity cases to the Circuit Family Court (s.38(2)). In addition s.39 clarified the requirements surrounding domicile and/or residence of a party or parties seeking a nullity order.

At the commencement of any application for a decree of nullity, there exists a presumption in favour of the validity of that marriage ceremony. This long-standing view has been repeatedly asserted, regarded by Fitzgibbon J. in *Mulhern v Cleary* [1930] I.R. 649 at 699 as "a very strong presumption" and was most recently confirmed in *AB v EB* [1997] 1 I.R. 305 per Budd J. Thus the onus is on the petitioner to rebut the presumption. There is an ongoing dispute as to the appropriate standard of proof applicable in nullity cases. The history of the debate is set out in the judgment of Budd J. in *AB v BB* [1994] 2 F.L.R. 36. In *AB v EB*, the burden of proof was regarded by Budd J. to be on the balance of probabilities. He rejected the suggestion that nullity suits should require a higher degree of proof than was required in other civil claims. In *Griffith v Griffith* [1944] I.R. 35 this onus was said to be "severe and heavy". Kenny J. in the Supreme Court in *S v S*, unreported, Supreme Court, July 1, 1976 stated that the petitioner must "remove all reasonable doubt" and establish her case "with a high degree of probability". However in the more liberal case of *N (orse K) v K* [1985] I.R. 733, McCarthy J. in the Supreme Court said that the petitioner had to prove his case "upon the balance of probabilities standard". There was evidence of judicial disagreement as to the standard of proof applicable in *UF (orse C) v JC* [1991] 2 I.R. 330 where the issue was ultimately reserved for determination at a future date. The existence of this confusion was recognised in the High Court by O'Higgins J. in the more recent case of *PF v GO'M (otherwise GF)* [2001] 3 I.R. 1, where he referred to the "considerable doubt as to ... the requisite standard of proof" in nullity proceedings and stated that clarification was awaited from an appropriate Supreme Court judgment. Whilst the general consensus is that a case must be proven on the civil standard, interestingly, Denham J. in *S v K*, unreported, High Court, July 2, 1992 was of the view that given the "constitutional protection of the institution of marriage", there exists a heavy burden of proof on the applicant, one of a "quasi-criminal trial nature".

Generally speaking the incapacity must exist at the time of entering into the marriage, but the party or parties do not necessarily have to be aware of its existence at that time. In *S v S* the intention not to have sexual intercourse existed at the time of the union, therefore the necessary consent to enter into the union was held not to exist. In all cases where the fact of the homosexuality of one of the parties was accepted as existing but unknown at the time of the union, the decree of nullity has been granted. No case has come before the courts where an orientation was developed after the union. In *UF (orse C) v JC* [1991] 2 I.R. 330, Finlay C.J. confirmed that proof that a person at the date of the marriage lacked the capacity to enter into and sustain a normal marital relationship constituted a valid ground for nullity. This need for the incapacity to exist at the time of the marriage is stated in the report of the Law Society of Ireland's Law Reform Committee, where they refer to *S v S*, unreported, Supreme Court, July 1, 1976, as an example of where a party may be deemed impotent even where the parties engaged in full sexual intercourse before the marriage.

Grounds for relief

(1) Absence of a full, free and informed consent

Proof of the absence of the full, free and informed consent of one or both of the parties to the marriage will cause the marriage to be declared void ab initio. This basis for nullity encompasses all forms of pressure and circumstances which might have vitiated the apparent consent to the marriage. The Supreme Court decision of *N (orse K) v K* [1985] I.R. 733 is in essence the birthplace of the judicial recognition of the requirement of a full, free and informed consent to the marriage ceremony. Finlay C.J. noted that the applicant was a quiet, unassertive girl who was not at the time of the marriage in a position, due to surrounding circumstances, to think clearly about the choices available. In such circumstances, her consent, if given, could only be regarded as apparent in nature. The petitioner had become pregnant at 19 years of age, following a short and casual relationship with the respondent. The decision to marry was taken by her parents who were ultimately held to have placed her under such duress that she was deprived of the capacity to enter into the marriage voluntarily. The Supreme Court confirmed that whilst there is a presumption that the marriage ceremony is valid, this can be rebutted by evidence of duress which has negated the consent of one or both of the parties. The court made it clear that imprudent or improper motives were not a ground upon which a nullity decree would be granted provided a decision reached by the parties "is truly their own decision" and a marriage cannot be impugned or annulled merely because it was later seen to be unwise. Although the judgments (both High Court and Supreme Court) are discussed below in the context of the ground of duress, the fact of the duress and the applicant's inability to freely exercise her independent will were deemed to prevent a valid marriage ceremony taking place.

Kinlen J. in *O'B v R* [1999] 4 I.R. 168 has recognised the undoubted "overlap between lack of consent by reasons of normal comprehension of the marriage contract and lack of consent due to duress". The presence of duress, whatever the source or cause is considered below, other circumstances preventing a full, free and informed consent to the marriage will be considered now.

In *MO'M v BO'C* [1996] 1 I.R. 208, Finlay C.J. stated that what has to be determined is whether the consent of the wife was an informed consent, a consent based upon adequate knowledge. It was confirmed by the court that the test is subjective in nature, with the ruling in this instance turning on whether the husband's prior attendance at a psychiatrist was a circumstance that would have influenced the petitioner's decision to consent to the marriage. It was held that his failure to provide her with this information deprived her of knowledge of a circumstance which was relevant to her decision. For this reason, her consent was not informed and the marriage was declared to be null and void. In *BJM v CM* [1996] 2 I.R. 574 the petitioner claimed to have been repelled by the respondent's physical condition, the extent of which was only revealed to him after the marriage had taken place. He claimed that as a direct result of his revulsion he was unable to maintain a marital relationship with the respondent and he sought a decree of nullity based on the lack of his full and free consent.

Flood J. stated that the respondent had been lacking in frankness and honesty in not revealing the extent of her scarring and disfigurement. As the petitioner was unaware of the full details of her injuries at the time of the marriage, he was deemed to have been deprived of a proper election. Accordingly his consent to the marriage was apparent rather than real.

In *PF v GO'M* [2001] 3 I.R. 1 the ever-expanding judicial approach to applications for nullity was pulled back and the court distinguished the earlier decision of *MO'M (otherwise O'C) v BO'C* [1996] 1 I.R. 208. McGuinness J. signalled a retrenchment of the generosity of the courts regarding the question of prior knowledge in the area of nullity law. At the time of the marriage, unknown to the applicant, the respondent was conducting an affair with a third party, K. In the High Court, O'Higgins J. refused to grant the decree of annulment, stating there was no obligation on the parties to disclose inappropriate behaviour prior to the marriage. McGuinness J. followed this approach on appeal, despite the argument by the petitioner that had he known his wife was having an affair during their engagement he would not have married her. The court was not willing to apply a purely subjective test, ruling that the requirement of full, free and informed consent should not be extended to cover concealed misconduct and other forms of misrepresentation. To do so, it was stated, "could bring uncertainty into a wide variety of marriages" which would be "undesirable as a matter of public policy". The Law Society report views this decision as a return to the traditional restrictive approach to the remedy of nullity. This conservative judicial approach has been evident in very recent decisions in the area of nullity law. It is certainly arguable that the courts feel less compelled to take a sympathetic approach to applications for nullity, given the availability of the remedy of divorce since 1997. The nullity decree was refused by O'Higgins J. in *LB v McC,* unreported, High Court, December 20, 2004, where the petitioner claimed that her consent was not fully informed and was obtained by misrepresentation of fundamental facts and fraud on the part of the respondent in respect of his personal circumstances, his family circumstances, his character and his intentions. Whilst the court once again accepted that the test to be applied is a subjective one, it would not accept that "lack of full disclosure about … financial affairs, family and social circumstances … [are] grounds on which one can base a claim for nullity". By contrast, O'Higgins J. noted that the successful application for nullity in *MO'M (otherwise O'C) v BO'C* [1996] 1 I.R. 208 had related to "considerations of inherent disposition and mental stability". In *AB v NC,* unreported, High Court, February 16, 2006, O'Higgins J. again refused the application for nullity, noting that at the time of the marriage, the question of the sexual orientation of the respondent was not an issue and thus could not be regarded as a circumstance of substance that might cause it to be declared void. Once again O'Higgins J. highlighted the significant distinction between information relating to inherent disposition and mental stability and that relating to misconduct or other misrepresentation.

(2) Duress

In *N (orse K) v K* [1986] I.L.R.M. 75, the Supreme Court, per Finlay C.J. emphasised that the voluntary consent of the parties to that marriage is essential for a marriage to be valid.

> "If ... the apparent decision to marry has been caused to such an extent by external pressure or influence, whether falsely or honestly applied, as to lose the character of a fully free act of that person's will, no valid marriage has occurred."

This notion was developed by the Supreme Court in *MO'M (orse O'C) v BO'C* [1996] 1 I.R. 208 where Blayney J. stated that for a consent to be valid it must be an "informed consent" based upon "adequate knowledge" of every circumstance "of substance" relevant to the decision made to marry. If a person marries as a result of fear, threats, intimidation, duress, undue influence or is perceived to have been under strain or pressure arising from surrounding circumstances such that the exercise of their independent will is prevented, the marriage will be deemed invalid.

The Irish courts awarded its first decree of nullity in *Griffith v Griffith* [1944] I.R. 35 primarily on the basis of fraud but considered the relevance of the duress placed on the petitioner prior to the marriage. Prior to the marriage he had been accused of having unlawful carnal knowledge of the respondent, ultimately causing her to become pregnant. He was threatened with criminal prosecution if he did not marry her. He claimed that the fear attaching to these circumstances caused him to go through with the marriage. Ultimately it was proven that the statement as to paternity was false and whilst the marriage was declared void, Haugh J. emphasised that had the allegation of paternity been true and the respondent induced by fear to marry the respondent, he would not have been willing to declare the marriage void on that basis alone. This position was rejected by the Supreme Court in *N (orse K) v K* [1986] I.L.R.M. 75 with the court taking the opportunity to state the law on this contentious ground for nullity. The petitioner sought a decree of annulment on the basis that she was forced to go through with the marital ceremony and that the duress placed on her by her parents and the respondent's parents was such to void the marriage for absence of real consent. Six weeks after the petitioner announced to her parents that she was pregnant, the marriage of the couple was agreed and organised in full by their respective parents. Although Carroll J. refused the order in the High Court, the Supreme Court rejected the pre-existing restrictive view of duress and advocated that it was not restricted to threats of physical harm or other harmful consequences.

In a 4:1 majority decision, McCarthy J. referred to the need for:

"a true voluntary consent based upon adequate knowledge and freed from vitiating factors commonly described as undue influence or duress, particularly those emanating from third parties".

This decision firmly established that a broad view is to be taken of the concept of duress in nullity petitions and that the more restrictive approach articulated in earlier cases is no longer a part of Irish law.

The source of the alleged duress was discussed by the Supreme Court in *B (orse O'R) v O'R* [1991] 1 I.R. 289 which supported the earlier views of the court in *N (orse K) v K* [1986] I.L.R.M. 75. The parties had married when the petitioner, aged 16, had discovered she was pregnant. She claimed that no attempt had been made to explain the alternatives to marriage, and she took no part in arranging her marriage to the respondent. The Supreme Court held in her favour, noting that she had received no advice either as to the nature of the covenant of marriage or as to any alternative courses of action she might take in the circumstances. Whilst in the High Court, Carroll J. refused to grant the relief sought, the Supreme Court regarded the petitioner as unable to freely exercise her independent will, making her consent merely apparent and not real. Similarly in the more recent case of *WD v CD*, unreported, High Court, April 3, 1998, Smith J. willingly granted the nullity sought where due to the arrival of a baby outside wedlock the petitioner claimed he had been placed under severe duress by both his parents and the respondent's parents to marry the respondent. Expert evidence was presented to the trial of the "overt and covert pressure from both families" which prevented the parties from availing of any time to consider the implications of marriage. The petitioner further claimed that he was neither financially nor emotionally ready for marriage. Relying upon the judgment of Finlay C.J. in *N (orse K) v K* [1986] I.L.R.M. 75, Smith J. declared himself to be "absolutely satisfied" that the decision to marry lost the character of a fully free act as a result of the external pressures from both families, and declared the marriage null and void.

Similarly in *AC v PJ* [1995] 2 I.R. 253, Barron J. was satisfied on the evidence that the petitioner's consent to the marriage was not a full and free exercise of her independent will, stating that the pressure imposed upon her was of a type that she was "constitutionally unable to withstand and which led inexorably to the marriage". The petitioner had become pregnant outside wedlock and although she did not want to marry the respondent, had felt dominated by him and had also feared her parents' reaction. The anxiety had resulted in her being admitted to a psychiatric hospital for treatment, and she was only discharged from hospital on the day before her wedding to the respondent.

A case concerning inter parte duress came before the courts in *PW v AO'C* [1992] I.L.R.M. 536. The petitioner claimed that the marriage of 35 years should be annulled because due to the respondent's actions, he had been pressurised into the marital ceremony. He claimed in evidence that the respondent had threatened to put her head in the oven or throw herself under a train if the marriage was delayed. In granting the decree of nullity, Blayney J. was satisfied that once the petitioner could show that the effect of the respondent's threats was to deprive his consent "of the necessary element of freedom required of a consent to marriage", and that pressure "continued to operate on the mind of petitioner right up to the time of the marriage", a decree of nullity could be ordered. He further stated that the nature of the duress was not an essential element, the fact of the duress was sufficient.

However there is clearly a very fine line between what will be regarded as real or apparent consent. In *O'S v W (orse O'S)*, unreported, High Court, July 25, 1989, the nullity was not granted, Costello J. stated that:

> "There is no evidence that she was a domineering sort of woman and whilst he took the threat of legal proceedings sufficiently seriously to cause him to consult a solicitor, the threat did not overbear his will to such an extent as to vitiate his ultimate consent".

Morris J. in *BC v LO'F (orse C)*, unreported, High Court, Morris J., November 25, 1994 declined to grant a decree as he did not accept that there was a lack of true consent despite acknowledging that "the parties are and were unsuited to each other" and their marriage "was a mistake from the start". However the court was not satisfied that the petitioner's free will was overborne by the facts and circumstances, and he was deemed to have given a true consent to the marriage.

(3) Impotence

Given the courts' willingness to develop the law of nullity based on emotional and psychological barriers to sustaining a normal marital relationship, far fewer cases have been brought before the courts based simply on physical incapacity to sustain a marital relationship. A decree of nullity for impotence is granted on the basis of a party's inability to sustain a normal marital relationship, physical intimacy being regarded as a fundamental aspect of that relationship. A marriage is regarded as consummated once the parties have engaged in "ordinary and complete" sexual intercourse after the solemnisation. (*D-e v Ag* (1845) 1 Rob. Eccl. 279). Thus it is argued that the physical incapacity of one of the parties to the marriage acts as an impediment to a normal marital relationship being sustained. However it is somewhat uncertain whether the courts will grant a nullity on the grounds of non-consummation arising from the wilful refusal of one of the parties. Kenny J. in *S v S*, unreported, Supreme Court, July 1, 1976 seems in favour of such an approach, granting the nullity sought by the wife in circumstances where the parties had not consummated the marriage as the husband had declared the marriage to have been a mistake from the beginning. Kenny J. accepted the respondent's unilateral repudiation of the marriage as a sufficient basis for the invalidation of the marriage. However the courts have more recently regarded the physical relationship between the parties as only one aspect of the relationship and it has been suggested that the lack of a consummated union may not in itself be sufficient to annul the marriage. Costello J. in *D v C* [1984] I.L.R.M. 173 emphasised the need to examine both aspects of the marital relationship, both the physical consummation and the emotional and psychological relationship between the spouses.

A decree was granted by the courts in *EC (orse M) v AM,* unreported, High Court, Barr J., December 5, 1990 where the marriage had not been consummated in circumstances where three years after the marriage ceremony the petitioner was diagnosed as suffering from a condition known as vaginismus which prevented her from having successful sexual relations with her husband. Barr J. required that the condition be incurable vis-à-vis the respondent but did not require the condition to be universal in nature. In addition he indicated that the petitioner's attempts to rely upon her own impotence were only successful because there was evidence that the husband had repudiated the marriage. The requirement of repudiation has since been rejected by the courts.

In more recent cases where there exists a difficulty with the physical relationship between the parties, it is more likely that the application for annulment will focus attention upon the emotional and psychological reasons for the physical difficulties, rather than rely entirely upon the lack of consummation, or ongoing physical difficulties between the parties to the marriage. Thus the courts' active involvement in developing the grounds upon which a nullity can be sought, and in particular their willingness to consider all aspects of the marital relationship has lessened the significance of the physical aspects of the union.

(4) Inability to enter into and sustain a normal marital relationship

This relatively new ground for nullity originated in the High Court case of *RSJ v JSJ* [1982] I.L.R.M. 263 and has since developed to encompass "sub grounds" which relate to the various physical and psychological reasons which might prevent a spouse from entering into and sustaining a normal marital relationship. Barrington J. was strongly of the view that whilst principles and rules were developed and established by the Ecclesiastical courts, this did not prevent the modern civil courts from developing those principles in light of developments in modern medicine. Although impotence had long been recognised as a physical impediment to a normal valid marriage, the courts became willing to draw an analogy with this long-standing ground when considering applications for annulments based on emotional or psychological impediments. Costello J. in *D v C* [1984] I.L.R.M. 173 confirmed that it is now possible to identify psychiatric illnesses, such as manic depression, which might be so severe as to prevent one of the parties from entering into and sustaining a normal marital relationship. In *UF (orse UC) v JC* [1991] 2 I.R. 330, the Supreme Court, per Finlay C.J. declared the fact of the husband's hidden homosexual nature at time of the marriage to be a valid ground for annulling the marriage as it caused him to be incapable of forming a normal marital relationship with the petitioner. The fact of this sexual inclination was sufficient and evidence of a psychiatric illness was unnecessary. Barrington J. in *RSJ v JSJ* [1982] I.L.R.M. 263 acknowledged that homosexuality was in fact a "much more serious impediment to marriage", which in his view would prevent any form of meaningful marriage, given that one party would lack entirely the capacity to enter into "a caring or even a considerate relationship with the other".

Psychological impediments to the capacity to enter into and sustain a normal marital relationship have also been considered by the courts. In *BJM v CM* [1996] 2 I.R. 574, Flood J. granted the nullity sought in circumstances where the applicant husband declared himself to be unable to maintain a normal marital relationship because of the psychological revulsion he felt towards his wife's physical appearance. Although the primary ground upon which the nullity was granted related to the absence of a full and free consent, the court was of the view that given his psychological revulsion, it was "improbable that he could maintain an emotional and psychological relationship such as is required to support a marriage." In *DK v TH*, unreported, High Court, O'Higgins J., February 25, 1998, per O'Higgins J. it was accepted by the court that the petitioner's history as a victim of sexual abuse placed him "in such an emotional and psychological state as to be quite incapable of entering into a marriage relationship". Similarly in *DMcC v EC*, unreported, High Court, McCracken J., July 6, 1998, the applicant's troubled history with alcohol and sexual abuse was deemed to have rendered him extremely immature as regards close relationships with others and he was regarded as "clearly not able to enjoy the type of relationship which marriage requires", and was thus deemed to be incapable of entering into or sustaining such a union with the respondent. The existence and effect of a personality disorder was considered by the High Court in both *GF v JB*, unreported, High Court, Murphy J., March 28, 2000 and *MOC v MOC*, unreported, High Court, Finlay Geoghegan J., July 10, 2003 and in each case was deemed to render the marriage void, given the consequential incapacity on the part of one of the spouses in each marriage. In the later case Finlay Geoghegan J. was satisfied that the required incapacity had been proven, noting the existence of "some inherent trait or characteristic in the personality of the person concerned, often referred to as a personality disorder". Conversely the fact of the respondent's alleged psychological immaturity and underdevelopment of character was regarded by O'Higgins J. as insufficient evidence of personality traits that might bring him "outside the norm". However even though evidence of one party suffering from bipolar disorder would not normally prevent capacity to enter into or sustain a normal marital relationship, in *O'K v O'K*, unreported, High Court, July 29, 2005, O'Higgins J. regarded the petitioner to be so incapable by reason of his illness and his personality. Thus the court examined the totality of the evidence when considering the capacity of the petitioner.

The high point of this jurisprudence is the decision of O'Hanlon J. in *PC v VC* [1990] 2 I.R. 90. In that case neither party suffered from a psychiatric condition but the court accepted from the evidence that there were elements of immaturity in the character and temperament of both the husband and wife which were such as to make it impossible to maintain a functional, viable marriage relationship with each other. That case involved a couple from the same social, educational and religious backgrounds.

They had both reasonably well-established careers and the wife was aged 26 and the husband 31 at the date of marriage. It was held as a fact that the wife had a particularly strong attachment to her mother and the evidence was that the couple failed to agree on even the most minor matters that arose in the course of their day-to-day life. The court accepted the evidence of the psychiatrist that the parties had an incapacity to adapt and adjust to one another and neither was "able to satisfy the emotional needs of the other".

In a far-reaching judgment, O'Hanlon J. held that:

"... the marriage was doomed from the outset by reason of elements of immaturity in the character and temperament of both husband and wife, and an inability on both sides to form and maintain a functional, viable marriage relationship with each other. There appears to have been a lack of capacity on each side to compromise, to give way, to adjust to the emotional needs of the other partner, and to reach a *modus vivendi* where a reasonable and tolerable marital relationship could evolve between them."

What O'Hanlon J. in *PC v VC* [1990] 2 I.R. 91 referred to as relational or subjective incapacity, has been somewhat diluted by later decisions of the court but it remains the seminal decision on the so-called "dysfunctional marriage". Recent judgments and in particular the judgment of Quirke J. in *PMcG v AF*, unreported, High Court, Quirke J., May 17, 2003 followed the decision of O'Hanlon J. and granted an annulment in a case where the parties lived together after the marriage for a relatively short time and in circumstances where there were almost constant disputes between them on even the most minor issue. Whilst neither party had a psychiatric illness, the petitioning husband had at the date of the marriage a state of mind which was "characterised by anger, disappointment, distress and frustration". The court expressly followed *PC v VC* [1990] 2 I.R. 91 and found that "by reason of factors connected with the personality and psychology of each partner it was impossible for them to sustain a normal marriage relationship for any length of time". In *FF v ED*, unreported, High Court, April 11, 2003, Murphy J. dismissed a petition for annulment on the grounds that while there was evidence from the medical inspector that the marriage relationship was not normal because of an immature personality and repetitive compulsion disorder on the part of the petitioner he did not believe that the marriage was doomed from the start, stating this to be a marriage that had broken down rather than one which had not existed. The court heard evidence that the couple scarcely lived together during their relatively short marriage, rather the wife continued to maintain her previous residence. The court heard evidence from the medical inspector that no normal marriage relationship existed to any significant degree because of the immature personality and some degree of a repetitive compulsion disorder on the part of the petitioner. However the court refused to grant a nullity, saying that it was not a marriage "doomed from the start." The court held that this was a marriage which had worked and had broken and that the degree of emotional or personality disorder was not such as to render the husband incapable of sustaining a normal marriage relationship. In particular the court said that while full-time living together may well be "a desirable and indeed important ingredient of family life" it was not an essential prerequisite to marriage particularly in contemporary marriages where both parties were in established careers at the date of marriage and as in this case where both of them were marrying for the second time.

In particular the court made the following comment:

> "It does not seem to me that the degree of emotional personality disorder, repetitive compulsion of the petitioner, nor indeed his idealised relationship, were of such a degree as to constitute an emotional immaturity rendering him incapable of sustaining a normal marriage relationship with the respondent. ... The evidence of medical inspector was that the petitioner was suffering from both an immature personality disorder and from a repetitive compulsion disorder only in relation to his relationship with and subsequent marriage to the respondent. I find that neither disorder prevent him entering into a marriage relationship with the respondent."

In *PC v CM*, unreported, High Court, Laffoy J., January 11, 1996 the court refused to grant a decree of annulment on the grounds of incapacity. The parties were married for approximately six years and had two planned pregnancies. There were intermittent periods of marital happiness but the petitioning husband sought an annulment on the grounds that a thread that ran through the marriage from the start to the finish was the respondent's relationship with the father of her child with whom she resumed a relationship during the currency of the marriage. The evidence of the psychiatrist called on behalf of the petitioning husband was that the respondent had an immature personality disorder that could not be cured or treated and which was caused as she developed and grew throughout her childhood and adolescence. This personality disorder was one characterised by an inability to make mature decisions and to act in a mature way and ipso facto to form a relationship and make decisions that are in the mutual interests of both. Laffoy J. took the view that the respondent had displayed in her life a degree of wilfulness and a strong personality and that the fact that she was unfaithful on two occasions in the course of the marriage did not arise because of some inherent trait which compelled her to do this but because she had wanted the sexual intimacy with those other persons. The court refused to grant a nulllity holding that a valid marriage had broken down and that the marriage was not void ab initio.

In *NC v KMcL*, unreported, Circuit Court, February 22, 2002, McMahon J. refused to grant the decree of nullity sought by the applicant. The couple had known one another since they were children and a child was born to the relationship before they married. They lived together for several years with their child and bought a house. During those years they spoke about marriage and it was clear on the evidence that they planned to marry at some stage in the future. They undertook a pre-marriage course and married when their son was four. They had sexual relations on their wedding night but no further sexual relations after thc marriage. Within three weeks of the marriage the respondent wife embarked on a sexual relationship with a friend and within a few months she was pregnant with her new partner's child and left the family home. There was no evidence from the psychiatrist who examined the parties that there was any inadequate or immature personality and the court seemed to take the view that even had such a finding been made it would have required proof of an inadequate or immature personality to an abnormal degree before granting an annulment. Counsel had argued that while there seemed to be a capacity to enter into a marriage in this case, there was no capacity on the part of the wife to sustain a marriage. Notwithstanding these representations, the annulment was refused.

In *LB v TMcC*, unreported, High Court, O'Higgins J., December 20, 2004, the petitioner sought a decree of annulment both on the grounds of her husband's alleged immature or underdeveloped personality and because the marriage was obtained by what she described as misrepresentation of a fundamental fact by the respondent of his personal circumstances, his character and his intentions. However, O'Higgins J. was not prepared to accept the alleged behaviour of the respondent was sufficient to persuade him that this personality defect was present. The failure of the respondent husband to be a bread winner for the family and to make full disclosure of his financial affairs, family and social circumstances were not such as to entitle the petitioning wife to a decree of annulment.

Bars to relief

Approbation and delay

Delay in presenting a petition is not an absolute bar to the remedy as was evident in the High Court decision of *GMcG v DW and AR* [2000] 1 I.R. 96. The reason for the delay is vital as a long delay may give rise to so heavy a burden of proof on the petitioner that he may be deprived of the remedy sought. The knowledge of the person during the delay is crucial as was discussed by Donovan L.J. in *Pettit v Pettit* [1962] 3 All E.R. 37 where it was stated that a delay could be excused if during the period of delay the petitioner was not aware of the remedy available to him. Otherwise a court may take the view that the marriage has been approbated. However, in *CM v EL (orse EM),* unreported, High Court, July 27, 1994, Barr J. granted a decree of nullity on the ground of a psychiatric illness 20 years after a couple married. The applicant in that case had only become aware of his legal rights shortly before issuing proceedings and thus was "guilty of no unconscionable delay".

In *O'B v R* [1999] 4 I.R. 168 the suggestion that the petitioner had unreasonably delayed in seeking the annulment order was rejected by the courts notwithstanding that the matter was heard almost 30 years after the marriage was solemnised. In addition the court rejected the suggestion that in seeking both maintenance from the respondent and social welfare payments based on her married status, the petitioner had approbated the marriage. Applying for social welfare for the support of herself and her child was not in the circumstances to be regarded as an approbation of the marriage. However, in *MJO'D v CDO'D,* unreported, High Court, May 8, 1992, O'Hanlon J. took a less sympathetic view of the petitioner who sought an order of the court declaring his marriage to the respondent to be null and void. Given that the applicant had been in receipt of legal advice since the early 1970s but chose to delay the instituting of proceedings for annulment, there was deemed to have been approbation of the marriage by him of such a character as would disqualify him from obtaining the relief sought.

Consequences of nullity order (including ancillary relief)

It has long been a contentious issue that parties to a void marriage can not seek financial support or property orders from the courts. The 1984 Law Reform Commission report on Nullity of Marriage recommended the introduction of judicial powers regarding property and maintenance rights of parties to an invalid marriage both in favour of the applicant spouse and/or children of the void union. Of course, maintenance can always be sought by one parent from the other in respect of a child, irrespective of the circumstances of the birth or the relationship between the parents. As regards the succession rights of the children of a void or voidable union, the Report recommended that they should have the same succession rights as children born to parents who are validly married but that conversely the parties to a void or voidable marriage that has been annulled should have no succession rights in each other's estate. The issue of ancillary relief in the context of nullity was also considered by the Law Society Law Reform Committee who favoured the making available to the courts, the right to make limited ancillary relief orders, to include restricted powers to make orders in respect of the family home. Such awards of ancillary relief should be decided upon and awarded on an equitable basis. The underlying objective would be to allow the financially weaker spouse to achieve financial independence where possible. Any such financial awards, it was suggested, should be finite in nature.

Canonical annulments

Although canonical annulments may be seen by many as a vital aspect of the nullity process, legally they have no effect. In other words, there is no greater right to remarry if a canonical annulment has been secured. Arguably however, obtaining a canonical annulment can be evidence of the repudiation of the marriage. In *O'B v R* [1999] 4 I.R. 168, Kinlen J. considered referring the fact of the petitioner's bigamy to the DPP. The marriage between the parties had previously been annulled by the Roman Catholic Church in 1977 and on foot of this she had remarried although no civil amendment had been secured. However on the facts, Kinlen J. found that the first marriage had in fact been invalid and was unable to determine whether this meant that she could not be prosecuted for bigamy. As the law was unclear on the point he declined to make any referral to the DPP.

Reform of nullity law

Two significant reports have been published in recent years considering the urgent need for the restatement and reform of nullity law. The Law Reform Commission published its report on Nullity of Marriage in 1984, recognising the lack of modern Irish jurisprudence in this area and the consequential difficulties for the law both in theory and practice. The Report sets out the existing grounds for annulment of marriage under Irish law but given the lack of a modern and consistent set of legal principles it ultimately details its recommendations for the significant reform of the law of nullity of marriage. More recently the Law Society of Ireland's Law Reform Committee has published a report entitled "Nullity of Marriage: The Case for Reform" (2001). As the title suggests, the Committee identifies nullity law as a priority area in need of reform. These report-based calls for reform have been echoed by the Irish courts, in his dissenting judgment in *N (orse K) v K* [1985] I.R. 733, Henchy J. highlighted the need for a:

"… modern Statute providing for the grant of decrees of nullity of marriage on fair, reasonable and clearly stated grounds and making due provision for the consequences of such decrees on those directly affected by them".

This was cited favourably by McGuinness J. in the subsequent Supreme Court ruling in *PF v GO'M (orse GF)*, unreported, Supreme Court, November 28, 2000 where she suggested that given the recent legislative focus on the remedies of judicial separation and divorce, it would be:

"… desirable for the Oireachtas to turn its mind to providing a clear statutory code setting out both the grounds for nullity and its ancillary consequences both for the parties and for any possible children".

In its report the Law Society Reform Committee proposed quite a drastic overhaul of the basis upon which a decree of nullity might be sought. In essence it called for the abolition of the grounds of impotence and inability to enter into and sustain a normal marital relationship, suggesting that such cases should be pleaded under the divorce jurisdiction. The Law Reform Commission in its earlier report considered the grounds of impotence and noted that incapacity on the part of a spouse to have sexual intercourse with his other spouse should invalidate the marriage. The Report advocated the removal of the existing limitations in respect of a party's capacity to rely upon their own impotence. It also confirmed the existing position regarding wilful refusal to consummate a marriage as an insufficient ground for annulment. However it should be noted that this currently can and is regarded as an evidentiary fact that might assist the court when ruling on a nullity based on the grounds such as the inability of a party to sustain a normal marital relationship. As regards the incapacity grounds generally, the report of the Law Reform Commission set out proposals for reform in respect of a number of aspects of that ground. The Report called for a stated ground to allow a marriage to be annulled where on application of one of the parties, it is shown that at the time of the marriage one spouse had so strong a homosexual orientation as to make it impossible for the couple to form a genuine life-long marriage relationship. Such circumstances arose in *UF v JC* [1991] 2 I.R. 330 where the Supreme Court confirmed that the incapacity of one party by virtue of a homosexual nature, to form or maintain a normal marital relationship with the other party, was a valid ground for a decree of annulment.

As regards mental capacity to enter into and sustain a normal marital relationship, the Report confirmed the longstanding position that a marriage will not be valid where one of the parties at the time of the marriage lacks sufficient mental capacity to understand the nature of the marriage contract and the obligations normally attaching to marriage. It cited several cases to illustrate the more liberal approach of the courts in recent years, including *RSJ v JSJ* [1982] I.L.R.M. 263 and *D v C* [1984] I.L.R.M. 173. In light of this vacillating position of the courts, the Report recommended an agreed formulation for this ground, as follows:

"A marriage should be invalid on the ground of want of mental capacity where, at the time of the marriage, either spouse is unable to understand the nature of marriage and it obligations or where a spouse enters a marriage when, at the time of the marriage, on account of his or her want of mental capacity, he or she is unable to discharge the essential obligations of marriage."

When considering the ground of duress, the Law Reform Commission Report firstly confirmed the existing position; that duress, exercised by the other party to the marriage or some third person, vitiates the consent of a party to a marriage, thereby causing the marriage to be invalid. However it further noted that judicial flexibility at the time of the writing of the report had evidenced a broadening of this ground, allowing previously unacceptable forms of threats or duress to represent sufficient grounds for the granting of an annulment. Consequently the Report recommended that the enactment of legislation to clarify the area was necessary, primarily to confirm that a petition for nullity of marriage based on duress should not be dismissed simply because a party married as a result of a "just threat". The related ground referred to in the Report as "fraud, mistake and non-disclosure" was also assessed with the Report commencing by confirming that "under present law fraud or mistake will render a marriage void only in very narrow circumstances – essentially where either party is misled or mistaken as to the nature of the ceremony or the identity of the other party". An expansion of this ground was called for, with the Report recommending that there "should also be a more general ground of fraud or mistake and that it should be a ground for annulment that a party was induced to enter into a marriage as a result of a fraudulent misrepresentation made by or on behalf of the other party to the marriage". It was also recommended that the following limited incidents of fraudulent non-disclosure should afford grounds for nullity:

(a) non-disclosure of an intention at the time of entering the marriage not to consummate the marriage;

(b) non-disclosure of an intention at the time of entering the marriage to desert the other partner immediately and permanently;

(c) non-disclosure of an unqualified intention never to have children with the other spouse, by reason of which the other spouse was induced to marry;

(d) non-disclosure of a known condition of permanent sterility, by reason of which the other spouse was induced to marry.

The urgent need for the reform of Irish nullity law has been highlighted repeatedly over the last 20 years by both the judiciary and those concerned with reform in the Irish legal system. As well as highlighting particular aspects of the law that need to be amended and updated, the general refrain has been that the law needs to be both codified and clearly stated as reliance upon purely judge-made law is far from satisfactory. The most recent call for the codification of the law of nullity came from the Law Society Reform Committee report in 2001, but as yet no legislative steps have been taken in this area.

3. MARITAL BREAKDOWN

Introduction

Typically, the intervention of the State in the marital union arises only when that union, or some fundamental aspect of it, ceases to function harmoniously. Whilst Irish law has never sought to directly dictate the roles and responsibilities of the parties to a marriage it has undoubtedly stated the nature and extent of the duties and obligations of spouses both to each other and to any children of the union upon the breakdown of the marriage. Thus the focus of the lawmakers has been on the regulation of spouses upon marital breakdown, such inter parte obligations being capable of surviving a decree of judicial separation or even divorce.

History of remedies

Prior to the introduction of the remedy of judicial separation in 1989, the options available to estranged spouses were very limited. A private arrangement could be made between the parties that could be made legally binding on the parties in the form of a separation agreement. Although such a remedy was limited in its scope, it represented a means of structuring and resolving many of the issues between the parties. There also existed the remedy of divorce *a mensa et thoro*, a remedy carried over from the Ecclesiastical courts which was available on limited grounds; adultery, cruelty and unnatural practices. The jurisdiction for this remedy passed to the High Court of Ireland by virtue of s.17 of the Courts of Justice Act 1924. In 1983 the Law Reform Commission was tasked with examining the existing law relating to divorce *a mensa et thoro* in light of the Constitutional protection of the marital family and to consider possible reforms of that law, without the necessity for a Constitutional referendum. The remedy of divorce *a mensa et thoro* did not dissolve the marital union nor entitle either party to remarry; rather it simply relieved the petitioner of his/her obligation to cohabit with the respondent party. The two main aspects of the report issued by the Law Reform Commission concerned the grounds for relief and the ancillary financial orders that could attach to a decree. The published report was very much reform-focused and considered in detail the best way forward for this remedy, which it regarded as more appropriately titled 'legal separation'.

CORK CITY LIBRARIES

Given the cost, the lack of financial relief and the limited availability of divorce *a mensa et thoro*, and in light of co-existing statutory provisions which empowered the courts to make orders providing for inter-spousal financial provision and relief from domestic violence, it was noted that the remedy of divorce *a mensa et thoro* was infrequently sought. Appendix two of the report details the statistics relating to proceedings for divorce *a mensa et thoro*. The last five years of the statistics included in the appendix illustrate most clearly the infrequent rate of application and very limited success in this context. From 1978–2002, 146 applications were made yet only 13 decrees were granted during that period.

Separation agreements

Introduction

Separation agreements are the long-standing tool utilised to regulate the relationship between spouses, often including the regulation of ongoing rights and obligations, notwithstanding the breakdown of the marriage relationship. Such an agreement would traditionally have included clauses dealing with the parties' agreement to live apart, a non-molestation clause, an agreement as to the custody and access of any children of the marriage, and the division and distribution of the assets of the parties, often to include a clause providing for the ongoing maintenance of the dependent spouse.

Separation agreements—not a bar to maintenance proceedings

The dependent spouse typically seeks to include a clause entitling her to maintenance from the financially stronger spouse. Maintenance is automatically payable in respect of children but whether it is also paid for the spouse depends upon the particular circumstances of each case. Maintenance can be payable weekly, fortnightly, monthly or annually, whatever is agreed between the parties, or can also take the form of capitalised payments. The terms of the separation agreement can include an express provision that it is subject to variation should the circumstances of the parties change. In any case the issue of maintenance can never be definitively agreed upon and is always subject to change. So even where a spouse covenants in the separation agreement that the issue of maintenance is settled in full and final agreement of the parties, he is still entitled to return to the courts with an application under s.5 of the Family Law (Maintenance of Spouses and Children) Act 1976 ("the 1976

Act"). Neither is any such order final as there exists a statutory right under s.6(1) of the 1976 Act which empowers the court to discharge or vary a maintenance order at any time after it is made.

However there are limitations to the execution of a separation agreement. Given that it is in essence a private arrangement between two persons it suffers from the lack of the force of a court order, unless it is registered under the 1976 Act, a procedure which is little used. A pension can only be varied or split in favour of a non-member spouse pursuant to a court order as the trustees of a pension scheme are not party to the separation agreement and thus are not bound by its contents. Finally where a default occurs in relation to an aspect of the agreement, the parties do not have recourse to the courts for contempt, rather the remedy lies in the more difficult breach of contract proceedings.

In *HD v PD*, unreported, Supreme Court, Walsh J., May 8, 1978, the petitioner wife had previously issued proceedings and these had been settled by way of agreement in 1973. The agreement provided inter alia that the respondent husband would pay to the wife the sum of £10,000 in "full satisfaction of all the claims in the petition". The case in issue arose from the issuing of further proceedings in 1977 by the wife under the terms of s.5 of the 1976 Act for the support of herself and two of her children. The husband claimed that she was estopped from succeeding with her claim by virtue of the consent signed in 1973. However the court held that under the provisions of s.5 of the 1976 Act, a maintenance order can be made by the court if it appears to the court that a spouse has failed to provide "such maintenance as is proper in the circumstances." Walsh J. was of the view that "it is not possible to contract out of the Act by an Agreement made after the Act came into force or by an agreement entered into before the legislation was enacted." However perhaps this case does not mean that the terms of any separation agreement can be over-turned rather it should be limited to its own facts as it relates to maintenance. Notwithstanding this, the principle was followed by Barr J. in the High Court case of *JH v RH* [1995] 3 Fam. L.J. 96 where he stated that the petitioning wife was entitled to ignore the provisions of the separation agreement which provided that the settlement was:

> "… a full and final settlement of all matters outstanding between them including any claim which the wife might have under the Judicial Separation and Family Law Reform Act 1989 or any amending legislation."

In the circumstances, the court made a maintenance order under s.5 of the 1976 Act. However where the court deems it proper it can equally refuse to make a subsequent maintenance order. In *OC v TC*, unreported, High Court, McMahon J., December 9, 1981, the wife issued fresh proceedings seeking maintenance for herself and her son, 11 years after the Supreme Court had disposed of the matter. In refusing to grant further payments McMahon J. stated that:

> "The wife's adultery with P, the terms of the deed of separation and her conduct since the separation amount to an unequivocal repudiation by her of any relationship with the husband. Her flagrant breaches of the terms of the separation deed and of the terms on which the Supreme Court awarded her custody ... damaged the husband in his relationship with these children. At the time the parties separated the wife became entitled to a large sum of money sufficient to make her financially independent for the remainder of her life. In these circumstances it would ... clearly be unfair to the husband to revive the obligation to support his wife which was extinguished by her adultery."

It is evident from this judgment that in order to succeed with a subsequent application for further maintenance a spouse must prove that she is in need of support. Interestingly it was decided in *D v D*, unreported, High Court, December 19, 1989, by Barron J. that it is open to the court to vary downwards a maintenance payment agreed in a separation agreement even where the separation agreement makes no provision for such variation. Equally in *MC v JC* [1982] I.L.R.M. 562, Costello J. held that an alimony agreement between spouses could, even in the absence of an express clause permitting review or variation, be varied so as to reduce the husband's liability. Costello J. rejected the argument that the court had no power to vary the husband's contractual obligations; although on hearing the financial evidence it declined to so vary.

Separation agreements as a bar to judicial separation proceedings

In *N(C) v N(R)* [1995] 1 Fam. L.J. 14 where the parties had entered into a separation agreement in 1986, McGuinness J. relied upon the express provisions of s.15(1)(c)–(d) and concluded that a separation agreement was not "of itself" a bar to the court's right to grant relief under the 1989 Act. She defended her decision by reference to existing English precedent and by reference to its necessity on grounds of public policy. It is arguable that in light of the real possibility of an unequal bargaining position it is essential that the court retain discretion to review these agreements. Despite representations by counsel for the respondent requesting finality, McGuinness J. noted that variability rather than finality is the general characteristic of family law matters. Thus she stated that setting it out in a separation agreement cannot make an agreement immune to this general principle of variability. She further strengthened her judgment by relying upon the Supreme Court judgment of Walsh J. in *HD v PD*, unreported, Supreme Court, Walsh J., May 8, 1978, where he emphatically stated that "it is not possible to contract out of the Act by an agreement". This remained the position until the decision of *PO'D v AO'D* [1998] 1 I.L.R.M. 543, a case stated to the Supreme Court from the Circuit Family Court by McGuinness J. The issue before the court was similar to that before the court in *N(C) v N(R)* [1995] 1 Fam. L.J. 14. Counsel for the respondent wife brought a motion before the Circuit Family Court seeking to an order for the proceedings issued by the husband to be dismissed by reason of the separation agreement signed between the parties in 1979. She argued that this estopped him from seeking an order under the 1989 Act. The questions posed by McGuinness J. in the case stated relevant to this discussion were as follows:

"1. Whether I was correct in holding that I had jurisdiction to grant a decree of judicial separation where a deed of separation existed which relieved each of the duty to cohabit with the other and where the parties had lived apart since the conclusion of the agreement.
2. Whether I was correct in holding that there was no estoppel by reason of the said [separation agreement] to prevent this court granting a decree of judicial separation pursuant to section 2 of the 1989 Act."

In delivering the decision of the Supreme Court, Keane J. relied upon the decision of Blayney J. in *F v F* [1995] 2 I.R. 354 where in similar circumstances a decree of judicial separation was deemed unnecessary as there was no longer an obligation to cohabit. Essentially the motivation for this decision was to prevent an injustice where one party could unilaterally repudiate the agreement by instituting proceedings under the 1989 Act.

Pre-existing separation agreements

Under s.20(3) of the Divorce Act, the court must take account of any separation agreement that may exist between the parties to the marriage in considering whether to make financial relief orders on divorce. Although the parties to the agreement may be contractually bound by its terms, given the underlying constitutional/statutory obligation to ensure that proper provision is made for the parties, the court is empowered under s.14 of the Divorce Act to disregard or even set aside any or all aspects of the agreement. The approach of the court has demonstrated a willingness to re-open matters, particularly where the separation agreement has been in place for some time. In any case the courts should never simply rubberstamp such an agreement without first considering its sufficiency, as is required under the Constitution and the Divorce Act.

Separation agreements not a bar to divorce proceedings

Prior to the introduction of divorce, the Irish courts had developed a strict view of attempts to re-open separation agreements and had effectively prohibited such claims for further financial relief. However, in light of the enactment of the Divorce Act it appears that all matters are subject to review by the courts upon the issuing of divorce proceedings. The extent to which the Irish courts have had regard to a pre-existing separation agreement between the parties to an application for a divorce will be considered further in the next chapter.

Judicial separation

Introduction

The enactment of the Judicial Separation and Family Law Reform Act 1989 ("the 1989 Act") gave rise to the introduction of a more accessible remedy of judicial separation and was regarded as a "watershed in Irish family law". (See Alan Shatter, *Shatter's Family Law*, 4th edn (Dublin: Butterworths, 1997) at 383). Perhaps most significantly the courts were now empowered to make orders for ancillary relief in respect of assets held legally or equitably by either spouse and such orders could be made at the discretion of the presiding judge whose primary task was to make whatever orders were necessary in the interests of justice. Shatter notes that the 1989 Act abolished the remedy of divorce *a mensa et thoro* and

"... put in place most of the ancillary relief orders envisaged by the government as forming part and parcel of the divorce legislation that it had promised to enact if a majority had voted for constitutional change in the 1986 referendum".

The enactment of the 1989 Act and the availability of a marital breakdown remedy to which significant ancillary relief orders could be attached represented a hugely significant development in Irish family law. The Act sought to codify the myriad of issues arising in the context of marital breakdown, which had previously been dealt with in an ad hoc, piecemeal manner by the legislature, necessitating multiple applications by a spouse who may have sought the courts intervention in respect of maintenance, property, domestic violence, custody and access. All matters could now be brought before the courts in conjunction with the application for a decree of judicial separation. Any difficulties or apparent shortfalls with the 1989 Act were quite promptly dealt with upon the enactment of the 1995 Act. A decree of judicial separation is now granted by the court under Pt I of the 1989 Act and ancillary relief is ordered under the improved provisions of Pt II of the 1995 Act. The 1992 Government White Paper regarded the provisions of the 1989 Act as "comprehensive" and tellingly many of its provisions, as amended by the 1995 Act, most especially in relation to ancillary relief, were mirrored in the provisions of the Divorce Act when eventually enacted.

Grounds for granting a decree of judicial separation

In enacting the 1989 Act, the legislature set out the list of grounds upon which the court could, if satisfied that one or more is proven, order a decree of judicial separation. Such a decree can be ordered based upon the wrongdoing of the respondent spouse, e.g. adultery or alternatively can be ordered without apportioning blame for wrongdoing, such as the lack of a normal marital relationship or the fact that the parties have lived apart for one or three years. Where the applicant is shown in evidence to be the cause of the lack of such normal marital relationship, this does not estop him/her from relying upon this ground. This approach can facilitate the ordering of judicial separation without the necessity of finding one party legally culpable for the breakdown.

Section 2(1)(a)–(f) of the 1989 Act sets out the six grounds upon which a decree of judicial separation can be granted:

a) that the respondent has committed adultery;
b) that the respondent has behaved in such a way that the applicant cannot reasonably be expected to live with the respondent;
c) that there has been desertion by the respondent of the applicant for a continuous period of at least one year immediately preceding the date of the application;

d) that the spouses have lived apart from one another for a continuous period of at least one year immediately preceding the date of the application and the respondent consents to a decree being granted;

e) that the spouses have lived apart from one another for a continuous period of at least three years immediately preceding the date of the application;

f) that the marriage has broken down to the extent that the court is satisfied in all the circumstances that a normal marital relationship has not existed between the spouses for a period of at least one year immediately preceding the date of the application.

The burden of proof rests with the applicant who must satisfy the court as to the fact of one or more of these grounds. Where such facts are deemed to be proven on the balance of probabilities, the court is obliged to grant a decree of judicial separation in respect of the spouses concerned. The court must further be satisfied under s.3(2) that any dependent children are provided for, and can give directions under s.11 of the 1964 Act where necessary (s.3(3) of the 1989 Act). Section 8(1) of the 1989 Act provides that where a decree of judicial separation is granted by the courts, it shall no longer be obligatory for the parties to cohabit.

Ancillary relief on judicial separation is ordered under Pt II of the 1995 Act which amended and significantly improved the scope of the court's powers under the 1989 Act. Arguably the most significant statutory development was in respect of the pension of each of the parties, with the Irish courts being empowered to make pension adjustment orders, as necessary, to ensure that the parties are properly provided for and that justice is achieved in the particular circumstances. As the ancillary relief orders on judicial separation almost mirror those available on divorce, the orders that can be made on both judicial separation and divorce, and the approach adopted by the courts will be examined together in the next chapter.

Divorce

Introduction

The lack of any available legal remedy for marital breakdown before 1989 can certainly not be regarded as evidence of a lack of marital breakdown at that time. Regrettably, comprehensive statistics regarding the prevalence of marital breakdown were unavailable for many years. At the time of the publication of the 1985 Report of the Joint Oireachtas Committee on

Marital Breakdown, it was noted that statistics in this area could only be garnished in respect of those who had had recourse to the courts or those relying upon categorised state financial welfare support. The 2001 ESRI research document by Fahey and Russell again noted the lack of comprehensive statistics on marriage breakdown in Ireland; rather the available statistics reflected the marital status of the people of Ireland. In this regard, the 1979 census recorded 8,000 separated/divorced people living in Ireland, whereas the 2006 census recorded 166,797 separated/ divorced people.

Following the failure of the 1984 referendum on divorce, a more pro-active governmental approach was apparent in the lead-up to the 1995 referendum on divorce. The unprecedented cross-party support for change in this area strengthened the power of the pro-divorce campaigners. In addition the more prepared and considered approach of the government to this socially contentious, if not divisive issue, resulted in many of the previously utilised fear tactics being dissolved through the dissemination of information to the public. In this regard, the Government published a draft Divorce Bill for public consideration and debate. The referendum was held on November 24, 2005 and was ultimately carried by a mere 9,114 votes, 50.28 per cent of the people voting supported the proposed amendment and 49.72 per cent of those voting opposed it. The divorce regime in Ireland is grounded primarily upon an amended constitutional provision and more comprehensively by the provisions of the Divorce Act. The effect of the amended Art.41.3.2 of the Constitution is to introduce the remedy of divorce to Irish family law whilst stating the basic criteria to be fulfilled prior to the granting of a decree of divorce. This is in turn supported by the lengthy and broadly drafted provisions of the Divorce Act which statutorily empowers the court to order a decree of divorce and in so doing affords the judiciary very extensive freedom in determining what orders to make, when an application for a decree of divorce and ancillary relief comes before the courts. It appears that the reasoning that underpinned such extensive discretionary powers was grounded in a legislative desire to protect and guarantee as much as possible, the rights of dependent spouses and children.

Divorce—the grounds to be satisfied

Section 5 of the Divorce Act and Art.41.3.2 provide that a court designated by law may grant a decree of divorce, where on application to it, by either spouse, it is satisfied that:

(a) at the date of the institution of the proceedings, the spouses have
    lived apart from one another for a period of, or periods amounting
    to, at least four years during the previous five years,

(b) there is no reasonable prospect of a reconciliation between the
    spouses, and

(c) such provision as the court considers proper having regard to the
    circumstances exists or will be made for the spouses and any
    dependent members of the family.

No element of fault needs to be proven by either party in order to
successfully apply for a decree of divorce. As a result it is very possible
for a divorce to be granted in circumstances even where one spouse is
absolutely opposed to it, as the applicant has a constitutional right to
divorce once the three requirements are satisfied. In such a case the
opposing spouse can argue that there is a reasonable prospect of reconciliation, but of course this can be disputed in evidence. Once these three
statutory/constitutional grounds are proven, the court is obliged to order
the decree of divorce.

Living apart

Section 5(1)(a) of the Divorce Act requires the parties, at the time of
issuing the proceedings, to have been living apart for four out of the
previous five years. The notion of living apart is not defined by statute and
was first introduced under the terms of s.2(1) of the 1989 Act as the basis
for a number of grounds upon which a decree of judicial separation could
be granted. By way of statutory explanation, s.2(3) states that:

> "spouses shall be treated as living apart from each other unless
> they are living with each other in the same household, and
> references to spouses living with each other shall be construed as
> references to their living with each other in the same household."

The first judicial guidance on the no-fault ground of "living apart" in Irish
divorce proceedings arose in *McA v McA* [2000] 2 I.L.R.M. 48. The
parties were married in October 1968. Difficulties arose and in September
1988 the respondent left the family home. He returned in 1991 to live
with the applicant and their two children, agreeing to pay the applicant
£750 per month, later increasing this sum to £1,000 per month. Whilst the
applicant stated that she was happy with his return and never considered

her marriage to be over, the respondent stated his primary motive for returning to the family home was to develop his relationship with his then 18-year-old son. The parties slept in separate bedrooms even when they went on holidays with the children. The applicant sought a decree of judicial separation and the respondent counterclaimed for a decree of divorce; the date of institution of divorce proceedings was August 16, 1999. The applicant contested the respondent's entitlement to a decree of divorce on the basis that they had not been living apart for four of the five years preceding the date of the institution of the proceedings. McCracken J., in considering the law on living apart, noted that the Divorce Act did not provide any definition or guidance, thus he sought assistance from highly persuasive precedents in the jurisdiction of England and Wales. He accepted the decision in *Santos v Santos* [1972] Fam. 247 as clearly expressing "the view that the intention of the parties is a very relevant matter in determining issues of whether they live apart or whether there has been desertion", agreeing with the views of Sachs J. that it is "... necessary to prove something more than that the husband and wife are physically separated."

McCracken J. accepted this approach in *McA v McA*. In recognising that just as there is a mental element to living apart other than mere physical separation so too is there more to living together than just being physically in the same house. In this case, the husband's return to the family home in 1991 was not activated by a desire to restart the marriage, but to develop his relationship with his children. Accordingly he had no mental or emotional attachment to the marriage, although he did live in the same house as the wife. They ate and holidayed together, though that was accepted to be in the interests of the children. McCracken J. stated that in relation to the test for living apart:

> "I do not think one can look solely at where the parties physically reside, or at their mental or intellectual attitude to the marriage. Both of these elements must be considered, and in conjunction with each other".

Proper provision

There exists both a statutory and Constitutional obligation on the Irish courts, when granting a decree of divorce to ensure that proper provision is made for the spouses and any dependent children. Failure to secure such a standard prohibits the ordering of a decree of divorce. Yet "proper provision" has not been defined in any part of the Divorce Act and it is for the court to decide in every case what constitutes proper provision in the circumstances. In addition, the Divorce Act was enacted in a manner that permits repeated applications to the courts for ancillary relief, not only at the time of the decree being granted but also at any time thereafter. In this way the legislature, whilst permitting the breaking of the marital ties, has sought to maintain the financial obligations and responsibilities of each spouse long beyond the grant of the decree of divorce. Whilst recent judicial pronouncements have suggested that a clean financial break may be available to parties to an "ample-resources" case (*T v T* [2002] 3 I.R. 334), a distinct lack of financial finality remains typical where the parties struggle to adequately finance two homes instead of one.

Counselling and mediation

Both the 1989 Act and the Divorce Act place a statutory obligation on solicitors advising parties who wish to seek an order of judicial separation or divorce from the court, to advise the client of the alternative remedies available to them. (Sections 5 and 6 of the 1995 Act and ss.6 and 7 of the Divorce Act). The duties on the solicitor are the same whether the client seeks a separation or divorce, except that when considering an application for a decree of divorce, it is open to the client to alternatively seek a decree of judicial separation. The solicitor is obliged, prior to issuing proceedings for whatever remedy is sought, to furnish the client with a list of qualified persons who might be in a position to assist with the mediation or reconciliation process.

Recognition of a foreign divorce

Although less significant an issue in Irish family law since the introduction of a domestic remedy of divorce in 1997, the recognition of foreign divorces has received considerable legislative and judicial attention both prior to and since the introduction of the domestic remedy of divorce. Under the common law rules the Irish courts were satisfied to recognise a foreign divorce if at the time of issuing the proceedings, both parties were domiciled in the country granting the divorce. The enactment of the Domicile and the Recognition of Foreign Divorces Act 1986 abolished the concept of the dependent domicile of a wife providing that the domicile of a married woman is an independent domicile and abolished the out-dated notion that upon marriage a woman acquires the domicile of her husband, and is during the subsistence of the marriage incapable of having any other domicile. As a result a foreign divorce could now be recognised by the Irish courts where only one of the parties to the marriage was domiciled in the country granting the decree of divorce. The decision in *GMcG v DW and AR* [2000] 1 I.R. 96 sought to amend the common law, pre-1986 position, to the view that one party being domiciled or residing in a jurisdiction for the legislatively required period under the laws of that jurisdiction is sufficient. However this decision of McGuinness J. was put in some doubt by the subsequent judgment of Kinlen J. in *GEC v JAC; JOC and AG*, unreported, High Court, Kinlen J., March 9, 2001 where he refused to recognise the divorce granted to the parties in England as whilst at the time of the application for divorce the applicant had resided in London for 10 years, neither party was domiciled in England at that time. Kinlen J. refused to recognise the decree, fearing the uncertainty that would arise if the basis of recognition introduced by the 1986 Act was retrospectively extended; such uncertainty would affect the status of couples who were party to pre-1986 divorces, previously believed not to be capable of recognition. Notwithstanding this judgment, Morris J. in *DT v FL* [2002] 2 I.L.R.M. 152 supported the judgment of McGuinness J. in *GMcG v DW and AR* [2000] 1 I.R. 96. However, he also limited the scope of expansion of the rules relating to recognition to those divorces granted prior to the enactment of the 1986 Act, therefore precluding its application to the case before him. He was of the view that he 1986 Act prevented an expansion in respect of those divorces granted after the Act came into force as the legislature had, from that point on, assumed jurisdiction in the matter.

> "I have no doubt however, that since it was open to the court in *McG. v. W.* (No. 1) [2000] 1 I.L.R.M. 107 to bring the common law in line with current policy it was correct to do so. I believe that if there was a jurisdiction still vested in me I should do so in this case. However, in my view the passing of the Act removes this jurisdiction from me."

Unfortunately, however, Morris J. did not address the decision of Kinlen J. in *GEC v JAC*, unreported, High Court, Kinlen J., March 9, 2001 thereby failing to deliver a judicial determination on these conflicting decisions.

The importance of the domicile of the parties was highlighted in *RB v AS (orse AB)*, unreported, High Court, February 28, 2001, where Lavan J. refused to recognise the divorce decree granted by the German Court between AS and WS as neither party was domiciled in Germany at the date of instituting the divorce proceedings. Both parties were domiciled in Ireland and neither had adopted a domicile of choice in Germany. In *DT v FL* [2002] 2 I.L.R.M. 152 both parties had a domicile of origin in Ireland. The family moved to Holland in 1987 to facilitate the respondent's employment but the applicant and children moved back to Ireland in 1992. The respondent obtained a decree of divorce in Holland in 1994 and its validity depended upon whether he had relinquished his Irish domicile of origin for a domicile of choice in Holland. Morris J. held that the onus was on the respondent to satisfy the court that he was domiciled in Holland and that in seeking to do so it was insufficient to merely show that he resided there for a prolonged period of time. Instead the respondent was required to adduce further evidence indicative of the permanent nature of his residence in Holland. In the circumstances, he was deemed to have failed to do so and the High Court refused to recognise the Dutch divorce.

In respect of ancillary financial relief, either party to a validly recognised foreign decree of divorce can apply to the Irish courts under Pt III of the 1995 Act for such orders. The court is empowered to make a variety of ancillary relief orders, similar in scope to those ordinarily made upon granting a decree of separation or divorce in an Irish court. Prior to making ancillary relief orders, the Irish court must be satisfied as to its jurisdiction to do so, and in accordance with s.27 at least one of the following requirements has been satisfied:

1. Either of the spouses was domiciled in the State on the date of application for an order under Pt III of the 1995 Act, or was so domiciled on the date on which the divorce or separation took effect in the other jurisdiction.
2. Either of the spouses was ordinarily resident in the State for a period of one year ending on either of the above relevant dates.
3. Either of the spouses had a beneficial interest in land situated in the State on the date of institution of the proceedings.

Once satisfied as to its jurisdictional capacity, the Irish court is obliged, under s.26 to have regard to the following:

"(*a*) the connection which the spouses concerned have with the State,
(*b*) the connection which the spouses have with the country or jurisdiction other than the State in which the marriage concerned was dissolved or in which they were legally separated,

(c) the connection which the spouses have with any country or jurisdiction other than the State,

(d) any financial benefit which the applicant or a dependent member of the family has received, or is likely to receive, in consequence of the divorce or legal separation concerned or by virtue of any agreement or the operation of the law of a country or jurisdiction other than the State,

(e) in a case where an order has been made by a court in a country or jurisdiction other than the State requiring a spouse, or the spouses, concerned to make any payment or transfer any property for the benefit of the applicant or a dependent member of the family, the financial relief given by the order and the extent to which the order has been complied with or is likely to be complied with,

(f) any right which the applicant or a dependent member of the family has, or has had, to apply for financial relief from a spouse or the spouses under the law of any country or jurisdiction other than the State and, if the applicant or dependent member of the family has omitted to exercise any such right, the reason for that omission,

(g) the availability in the State of any property in respect of which a relief order in favour of the applicant or dependent member of the family could be made,

(h) the extent to which the relief order is likely to be enforceable,

(i) the length of time which has elapsed since the date of the divorce or legal separation concerned."

The case of *MR v PR* [2005] 2 I.R. 618 concerned the operation of Pt III of the 1995 Act and serves to illustrate the discretion and the scope of the powers available to an Irish court on foot of such an application. The parties had secured a divorce in Spain in 1996 with the husband paying the wife a lump sum of £50,000 in full and final satisfaction of her maintenance requirements. The wife subsequently discovered that the husband was the beneficiary of a trust valued at €2,900,000 and came before the Irish courts seeking further relief. Relying upon the English decision of *Holmes v Holmes* [1989] Fam. 47, Quirke J. was of the view that whilst he was not permitted to "review the correctness or rectify the decision of the foreign court", it was appropriate for an Irish court to intervene in "exceptional circumstances" where the result of the foreign proceedings had rendered an "unfair or unjust" state of affairs. More recently, in *PWY v PC*, unreported, High Court, Sheehan J., November 23, 2007, the applicant (former) wife sought, in light of the existing decree of divorce granted by the Hong Kong court, (inter alia) relief pursuant to Pt III of the 1995 Act. Ultimately the court refused the orders sought by the wife, declaring the Hong Kong court as the appropriate venue for such an application.

4. ANCILLARY RELIEF ON MARITAL BREAKDOWN

Introduction

Part II of the Family Law Act and Pt III of the Divorce Act grant wide-ranging powers to the court to make one or more of an extensive array of orders to provide for the financial needs of the applicant, respondent and any dependent members of the family. The breadth of judicial powers in separation/divorce proceedings is apparent in the governing legislative provisions; all assets held legally or equitably by one or both spouses can be considered for division and it is open to either spouse to apply for ancillary relief at the time of making the initial application or defence and counterclaim, or at any time after the decree is granted save where the proposed applicant has re-married. Once any such application is before the court, the presiding judge is entitled to make whatever order he considers appropriate, once he is satisfied that "… it would be in the interest of justice to do so" (s.16(5) of the 1995 Act, s.20(5) of the Divorce Act). The task for the court is to order a decree once it is satisfied that the welfare of the dependent children is provided for (s.3(2) of the 1989 Act) or that proper provision has been made for the parties (s.5 of the Divorce Act). The court has a wide discretion in relation to the division of the assets; proof of financial contribution is only one factor for the court to take into account under s.16 of the 1995 Act and s.20 of the Divorce Act.

Preliminary relief

Preliminary or interlocutory relief orders can be made by the court in the context of judicial separation proceedings under s.6 of the 1995 Act and in the context of divorce proceedings under s.11 of the Divorce Act. These provisions permit the making of preliminary orders after the issuing of proceedings but at any time prior to the hearing of the matter, as follows:

- a safety order, a barring order, an interim barring order or a protection order under the Domestic Violence Act 1996,
- an order under s.11 of the Guardianship of Infants Act 1964,
- an order under s.5 or s.9 of the Family Home Protection Act 1976.

Section 7 of the 1995 Act and s.12 of the Divorce Act deal with the right of the court to make orders for the payment of maintenance pending the hearing of the action. Such an order remains in force until the substantive matter is heard by the court. An order made under either of these sections can have attached to it, any terms and conditions as the court sees proper.

Division of Property

Factors to be considered by the courts

Introduction

Legislative direction for the judiciary is far from comprehensive in both the 1995 Act and in the Divorce Act. The terms of s.16/s.20 do not contain any guidance but rather provide the court with an objective, in that it requires the court, when making virtually any order for ancillary relief, and in determining the provisions of any such orders, to ensure that proper provision is made for the spouses and any dependent member of the family. The provisions of s.20(1) of the Divorce Act relate to orders made by the courts under ss.12, 13, 14, 15(1)(a), 16, 17, 18 and 22 of the Divorce Act. The focus of this section will be on the legislative provisions and case law governing the factors to influence the ancillary relief orders made in divorce proceedings. Whilst in divorce hearings the court will be influenced by issues such as the second family and perhaps a greater need for clean break between the parties, in essence the similar statutory provisions on separation and divorce will likely give rise to much the same interpretation and application of s.16 of the 1995 Act and s.20 of the Divorce Act.

Statutory factors for consideration

Whilst proper provision is a pre-requisite for the granting of a decree and thus might be regarded as an objective of the process, the failure to identify what might constitute proper provision and how it might be calculated in any given circumstances, certainly weakens its possible status as a legislative objective. Notwithstanding the generality of that requirement, s.20(2) of the Divorce Act requires in particular, that the court have regard to the matters contained in s.(20)(2)(a)–(l). This subsection refers to the following list of 12 factors, to which the court is to pay particular regard and it is for the trial judge to decide what weight is to be given to each of them in the individual circumstances:

a) the income, earning capacity, property and other financial resources which each of the spouses concerned has or is likely to have in the foreseeable future;

b) the financial needs, obligations and responsibilities which each of the spouses has or is likely to have in the foreseeable future (whether in the case of the remarriage of the spouse or otherwise);

c) the standard of living enjoyed by the family concerned before the proceedings were instituted or before the spouses commenced to live apart from one another, as the case may be;

d) the age of each of the spouses, the duration of their marriage and the length of time during which the spouses lived with one another;

e) any physical or mental disability of either of the spouses;

f) the contributions which each of the spouse has made or is likely in the foreseeable future to make to the welfare of the family, including any contribution made by each of them to the income, earning capacity, property and financial resources of the other spouse and any contribution made by either of them by looking after the home or caring for the family;

g) the effect on the earning capacity on each of the spouses of the marital responsibilities assumed by each during the period when they lived with one another and, in particular, the degree to which the future earning capacity of a spouse is impaired by reason of that spouse having relinquished or foregone the opportunity of remunerative activity in order to look after the home or care for the family;

h) any income or benefits to which either of the spouses is entitled by or under statute;

i) the conduct of each of the spouses, if that conduct is such that in the opinion of the court it would in all the circumstances of the case be unjust to disregard it;

j) the accommodation needs of either of the spouses;

k) the value to each of the spouses of any benefit (for example, a benefit under a pension scheme) which by reason of the decree of divorce concerned, that spouse will forfeit the opportunity or possibility of acquiring; and

l) the rights of any person other than the spouses but including a person to whom either spouse is remarried.

The precise status of these statutory factors is unclear. Whilst s.20(1) requires the court to "in particular have regard" to these criteria, suggesting that the 12 factors are one possible source of influence for the decision(s) of the courts, there is no express mandatory obligation to apply each factor to the circumstances of a case before the courts. This is evident from the reported judgments which illustrate varying levels of judicial references to aspects of s.20(1)(a)–(l). Thus it is arguable that the courts are permitted to exercise a significant discretion in dividing the assets of the parties before the court and are merely guided by these factors, as relevant. McGuinness J. has stated the position strongly, regarding the section 20 factors as "mandatory" and suggesting that there is an obligation on the judiciary to account, in light of the statutory factors, for any exercise of discretion (*MK v JP (orse SK)* [2001] 3 I.R. 371). Thus the impact of these 12 statutory factors differs depending not only on the facts of the case, but also on the attitude and approach of the presiding judge.

Section 20(4) is similar to s.20(2) in that it sets out specific criteria to be considered by the court when considering whether to make any orders in favour of a dependent member of the family:

- the financial needs of the member,
- the income, earning capacity, (if any), property and other financial resources of the member,
- any physical or mental disability of the member,
- any income or benefits to which the member is entitled by or under statute,
- the manner in which the member was being and in which the spouses concerned anticipated that the member would be educated or trained,
- the matter specified in paragraphs (a), (b) and (c) of subsection (2) and in subsection (3), and
- the accommodation needs of the member.

Whilst these criteria will be relevant where the court intends to make an order in favour of a dependent child, they can influence any of the orders that will be made, in so far as any financial relief order has the potential to impact upon dependent members of the family. This was evident in the High Court case of *EP v CP*, unreported, High Court, McGuinness J., November 27, 1998 where orders were made transferring the family home into the sole name of the applicant, and the sale of a second property held in the respondent's sole name, which were deemed necessary by McGuinness J. for the security and welfare of the children, as their need for a secure home was the most important aspect of the case. Although McGuinness J. admitted that she made the order for sale regretfully, she felt compelled to do so, in consideration of the interests of the children.

Factors to be considered by the court—case law

In *MK v JP (otherwise SK)* [2001] 3 I.R. 371 at first instance, Lavan J. relied upon both the common law principle that a husband should maintain his wife, and "... the fundamental rules that had been in existence for nearly 200 years in determining whether a wife is entitled to be maintained according to the style of her husband." This reliance upon common law rules of obligation together with judicially based notions of equality of division, appeared to ignore the Irish statutory regime in relation to the regulation of marital breakdown. However on appeal, McGuinness J. was quite convinced that the implied judicial discretion is not to be exercised at large, and that the terms of s.20 of the Divorce Act set out mandatory guidelines to which the courts must have regard:

> "... measuring their relevance and weight according to the facts
> of the individual case ... a judge should give reasons for the way
> in which his or her discretion has been exercised in the light of
> the statutory guidelines." (at 384)

In adopting this view, McGuinness J. considered that Lavan J. had notably failed to take these steps. Not only was the separation agreement relevant but so too, under the terms of s.20(2)(a)–(l) were many other factors, including that the couple had lived apart for 20 years, the wife's financial needs, the role she played in caring for the children and the fact that the entire of the husband's wealth has been accumulated subsequent to the separation of the parties.

In the body of her judgment, McGuinness J. set out almost the entire provisions of s.20, and referred to a number of cases where the terms of s.20 had already been considered (*JD v DD* [1997] 3 I.R. 64; *McA v McA* [2000] 2 I.L.R.M. 48; *JCN v RTN* [1999] I.E.H.C. 83 and *MG v MG*, unreported, Circuit Family Court, Buckley J., July 25, 2000). Although McGuinness J. acknowledged that the provisions of the Divorce Act "leave a considerable area of discretion to the Court in making financial provision for spouses in divorce cases", this discretion the learned judge opined, is "not to be exercised at large". Although discretion is exercisable on the part of the court, it is only so exercisable within the confines of the statutory guidelines set out by the legislature, referred to by McGuinness J. as "mandatory guidelines". In her judgment McGuinness J. stated that:

> "The court must have regard to all the factors set out in s. 20,
> measuring their relevance and weight according to the facts of the

original case. In giving the decision of the court, a judge should give reasons for the way in which his or her discretion has been exercised in the light of the statutory guidelines. In his judgment in the instant case the trial judge has notably failed to do this."

As a result, McGuinness J. felt compelled to return the matter to the High Court to be reconsidered. The matter was re-heard as *K v K* by the High Court before O'Neill J. (unreported, High Court, January 24, 2003) who ordered a significant reduction in the award made by Lavan J. and in so doing made extensive references to aspects of s.20. In taking the separation agreement into account O'Neill J. stated that he was of the view that it had failed to make proper provision for the applicant. He was further of the opinion that he was entitled to vary its terms and provide for the applicant spouse in circumstances where she had not been adequately catered for by the terms of the agreement. Notwithstanding the existence of a written agreement, negotiated by or on behalf of the two parties, O'Neill J. was willing to permit the renegotiation or reordering of what was previously regarded as a binding full and final settlement. The Supreme Court judgment in this case reflects the position previously taken by McGuinness J. regarding the impact of the equivalent s.16 factors under the 1995 Act. In the earlier judicial separation case of *JD v DD* [1997] 3 I.R. 64, it was noted by McGuinness J. that when calculating the appropriate lump sum and/or periodic payment orders to be made, "… full regard, of course, must be paid to the guidelines set out in s.16 of the Act of 1995." However even given these guidelines, the court still has "a wide area of discretion particularly in cases where there are considerable financial assets".

These views in relation to the correct judicial interpretation of s.20 were widely accepted and followed by the Irish judiciary. O'Donovan J. in the High Court in *CO'R v MO'R* [2001] 2 I.J.F.L. 24 considered the criteria to be applied by the court and when considering the orders to be made in relation to the family home, he noted that there exists a duty on the court to have regard to the welfare of the children and to the relative circumstances of the spouses, such that the ancillary relief would enable them to follow a lifestyle appropriate having regard to their means and prospects and their lifestyle while living together, and having regard to their age and the length of the marriage.

O'Sullivan J. in *CF v CF*, unreported, High Court, June 11, 2002 expressly approved of the views of McGuinness J. He further noted that he was guided primarily by the requirements of the statute and thus in his judgment he cited in full, the lengthy provisions of ss.16(1) and 16(2). However having quoted these two subsections in full, O'Sullivan J. did not consider them any further in his judgment nor did he apply them to the facts before him. As a result it is not possible to establish whether each factor was in itself influential to the outcome of the case or whether he was selective in applying certain factors. However he did recognise the more general requirements of s.16(5) when noting that he was under an obligation to ensure that:

"... the court shall not make any order under a provision referred to in subsection (1) unless it would be in the interest of justice to do so."

In *PO'D v JO'D*, unreported, High Court, March 31, 2000, Budd J. regarded the judgment of McGuinness J. in *JD v DD* as "a helpful review of the law and the relevant provisions governing the situation ...". Interestingly, in a similar approach to that adopted by McGuinness J., Budd J. thought it appropriate to cite in full the terms of s.16(2). In so doing he noted the compulsory obligation on the court to pay "full regard" to the guidelines contained in s.16, when making the "necessary calculations".

The views enunciated by McGuinness J. regarding the obligation on the judiciary to account for the basis of the decision made, has not always been shared by her colleagues. In relation to the apparent obligation to identify the factors which influenced the mind of the trial judge in question, in the judicial separation case of *AK v PK*, unreported, High Court, March 13, 2000 Murphy J. made a number of orders, including a periodical payments order, a property adjustment order, a right of residence and a preservation of pensions entitlement order without making any reference in his judgment to s.16 or to the factors contained therein that he believed to be relevant. This judgment is evidence of the danger of including a "catch-all" clause such as s.20(5) which can lead to and even permit the making of any order on the obvious basis of "necessity of justice".

More recently, the Supreme Court has considered the role and impact of s.20 in the ordering of ancillary relief on divorce in *T v T* [2003] 1 I.L.R.M. 321. Keane C.J. in acknowledging the detail of s.20(2) immediately recognised the broad discretion that this necessarily affords the judiciary in cases where the parties are unable to agree a settlement and he accepted that such breadth of discretion will unavoidably give rise to elements of inconsistency:

"... it is obvious that the circumstances of individual cases will vary so widely that ultimately, where the parties are unable to agree, the trial judge must be regarded as having a relatively broad discretion in reaching what he or she considers a just resolution in the circumstances. While an appellate court will inevitably endeavor, so far as it can, to ensure consistency in the approach of trial judges, it is also bound to give reasonable latitude to the trial judge in the exercise of that discretion." (at 24)

With reference to the judgment of Lord Hoffmann in the English case *Piglowski v Piglowski* [1999] 1 W.L.R. 1360, Keane C.J. confirmed that the view that there is no hierarchy of factors does constitute a part of Irish law. Notwithstanding this however, Keane C.J. also accepted that in the traditional case of a lack of significant assets, the first task of the court must almost certainly be to consider the financial needs of the spouses and dependent children. Equally, he recognised that where one spouse is working and the other spouse has taken on the role of homemaker, s.20(2)(f), which relates to contributions in the home environment, must be regarded as a relevant factor. In this regard, Denham J. was of the view that there exists a requirement on the court to take into account the work of the spouse in the home, such recognition being in line with the acknowledgment in the Irish Constitution of the importance of work done by women in the home.

"In this case the learned trial judge assessed correctly the family role of the respondent and gave a significant weighting for her time spent in the home. A long, lasting marriage, especially in the primary childbearing and rearing of a woman's life carries significant weight, especially if the woman has been the major home family carer."

In the High Court decision of *C v C*, unreported, High Court, July 25, 2005, O'Higgins J. noted that the law has set out "very specific statutory guidance" to assess what constitutes proper provision in any given case. However given the varying circumstances of cases he highlighted the importance of co-existing judicial discretion. He relied upon *T v T* [2003] 1 I.L.R.M. 321 to support this view and also the aforementioned position regarding a lack of hierarchy amongst the factors set out in s.20(2(a)–(l). Similarly, in the context of an application for ancillary relief where the parties had previously secured a foreign divorce, Quirke J. in *MR v PR*

[2005] 2 I.R. 618 considered in detail the wording and impact of s.16 of the 1995 Act. He identified ss.16(2)(a), (b), (c), (d), (f) and (l) as relevant in the circumstances of the case before him. This is an interesting approach and certainly Quirke J. did not shy away from the clear identification of those factors deemed relevant in the circumstances. He proceeded to discuss briefly the facts of the case with general references to those subsections, concluding that the applicant was thus entitled to the ancillary relief sought. Ultimately Quirke J. was of the view that he was alleviating the present inequitable financial circumstances of the parties "in a just and equitable fashion." He concluded the point by noting that the court would grant the ancillary relief sought on the basis of taking into account the statutory factors as required by law, and the fact of the respondent's obligation to contribute to the upkeep of his now estranged spouse and two children.

Pre-existing separation agreement

More generally s.20(3) of the Divorce Act requires the court in deciding whether to make an order for ancillary relief, to have regard to the terms of any separation agreement which has been entered into by the spouses and is still in force. On the basis of a literal interpretation, this is the only element of s.20 to place a mandatory obligation on the courts. However, the extent of the impact of such an existing agreement is uncertain, s.20(3) does not require the court to enforce its terms, rather it simply requires it to "have regard" to its contents. Couching the court's obligations in respect of a pre-existing separation agreement in this manner empowers the court to decide without any further guidance, the extent of the regard it will have for the agreement. Arguably the court could "have regard" to its terms and in so doing, decide to ignore it entirely or equally could strictly enforce them. This statutory approach does nothing to inform the parties of the likely impact of such a pre-existing agreement. The basis upon which this decision is made has not been ordered or assisted by the legislature as the Divorce Act adds nothing further to the issue. Rather it is a matter left entirely for the courts to determine in a given case. Such judicial discretion might be more fairly exercised if the legislature in drafting the Act had adopted a position on the significance of a pre-existing inter-spousal contract and indicated the relative value, even in broad terms, to be attached to such a significant agreement. The lack of clearer legislative guidance impacts particularly in the Irish context, where there has traditionally been significant reliance upon separation agreements and private ordering to regulate matters by private contract, given the lack of statutory remedy for separation and/or divorce. The difficulties arsing from the generality of s.20(3) is evident in the case law since the enactment of the Divorce Act which illustrates radically different judicial approaches to their relevance and impact on subsequent applications for ancillary relief on divorce. These varying judicial approaches to the impact of s.20(3) will be considered below.

In a manner similar to that in *C v C*, unreported, High Court, O'Higgins J., July 25, 2005, O'Higgins J. in *MP v AP*, unreported, High Court, March 2, 2005, having considered the 12 factors set out in s.20(2)(a)–(l), considered the relevance and impact of s.20(3), given the pre-existing separation order in this case. With reference to s.20(3) generally, O'Higgins J. noted that the weight to be attached to a prior settlement between the parties would vary from case to case, depending on many factors, but specifically mentioned the length of time since it had been compromised, the financial background of the parties at that time when compared with current financial circumstances, and their reasonable expectations at that time. Even in identifying these particularly relevant aspects of a separation agreement, O'Higgins J. noted that their influence would also vary depending on the circumstances of a case. In this case however, O'Higgins J. was of the view that the terms of the prior separation order "are of very great importance". Given the intention for the settlement to be "long term and lasting", the fact that the bulk of the family assets were transferred to the applicant and that the circumstances had not changed from what they were anticipated to be post the settlement, O'Higgins J. did not regard it necessary to make any property orders, notwithstanding a significant economic disparity between the parties. He did however vary maintenance upwards in favour of the applicant. The separation order and its contents did limit greatly the success of the applicant wife in this case who was regarded as being effectively and almost properly provided for under its terms. O'Higgins J. further suggested that in drafting s.20 in such a broad manner, the Oireachtas had "studiously avoided giving any prescriptive guidelines" to the court, leaving instead a broad judicial discretion.

More recently in *WA v MA* [2005] 1 I.R. 1, Hardiman J. took a radically different view in delivering a judgment which focussed primarily on the pre-existing separation agreement between the parties. With reference to both s.20(3) and the over-arching requirement of s.20(5) that justice be done, Hardiman J. distinguished the decision of O'Neill J. in *MK v JP (otherwise SK)* [2001] 3 I.R. 371 on a number of grounds:

- Length of time that had passed since the signing of the agreement
- Execution of agreement post the enactment of the 1989 Act
- Different personal and domestic circumstances of the parties
- Length of disconnection between the spouses

In addition Hardiman J. recognised the need to 'factor' into the consideration, the "twelve matters set out" in s.20(2). He carried out this exercise, albeit briefly, concluding that justice required him to make no further orders for ancillary relief. Interestingly, Hardiman J. was of the view that he was statutorily prevented from doing so by virtue of the terms of s.20(5).

In *CD v PD*, unreported, High Court, O'Higgins J., March 15, 2006, involving an application for judicial separation with ancillary relief, O'Higgins J. noted that whilst the court must take all the circumstances of the case into account it is specifically obliged to have regard to" the factors set out in s.16(2)(a)–(l). He emphasised the over-arching "proper provision" requirement, noting the ultimate test to be one of fairness, not equality. In order to achieve fairness, he pointed to the need to take the statutory factors into account, but equally noted the relative importance of each factor varying, depending upon the circumstances of the case. He reiterated his view that there is no hierarchy of importance to be attached to the "various factors".

Finally in *RG v CG* [2005] 2 I.R. 418, the court was of the view that the consent order was just one factor to be taken into account. In concluding her judgment, Finlay Geoghegan J. stated that one of the influencing factors was s.20 of the Divorce Act in light of all the circumstances of the family in question. However, she did not set out any detail (statutory provision or application to the circumstances of the case) relating to s.20(2)(a)–(l). It appears that her decision was reached on a more general assessment of the circumstances of the parties.

Full and final settlement clause in separation agreement

The weight being given to clauses in pre-existing separation agreements where such clauses seek to declare the agreement between the parties to be in full and final settlement of all matters, has varied considerably depending upon the approach of the presiding judge. Thus in *WA v MA* [2005] 1 I.R. 1, Hardiman J. regarded it appropriate to give "very significant weight" to the terms of the separation agreement and ultimately refused to order any further financial relief for the applicant wife. Alternatively in *RG v CG* [2005] 2 I.R. 418 the obligation to ensure that proper provision is made for the parties on granting the decree of divorce compelled Finlay Geoghegan J. to make further orders in respect of the applicant spouse. It is arguable that in *SJN v PCO'D*, unreported, High Court, Abbott J., November 29, 2006, Abbott J. in making additional orders in favour of the less wealthy husband, was quite tied by the terms of the five-year-old judicial separation order. Had it not existed it is reasonable to presume that the husband would have received a far more substantial share of the wife's assets and net worth. In the circumstances, he was awarded a lump sum of €2.15 million. In *SMcM v MMcM*, unreported, High Court, Abbott J., November 29, 2006, the applicant wife sought further ancillary relief notwithstanding the existence of a 15-year-old separation agreement which included a full and final settlement clause. Although he regarded the separation agreement as reasonable in the circumstances, Abbott J. was of the view that it would be unfair to rely upon the agreement in order to prevent the wife from enjoying a better standard of living and lifestyle generally, akin to that experienced throughout the country generally, and more specifically by the husband. Notwithstanding this however, Abbott J. acknowledged that his making of orders would equally be limited by the terms and fact of the separation agreement. Ultimately he increased the annual maintenance from €25,000 to €90,000 and ordered the payment of a lump sum of €400,000. In addition he ordered the division of the husband's pension to provide a retirement sum for the wife to the value of €1.25million. Thus although the courts have acknowledged the fact and significance of pre-existing separation agreements, particularly where they include a full and final settlement clause, this has more typically not prevented the court from making significant additional orders for financial relief, in light of the circumstances at the time of granting the decree of divorce.

The issue of the right to return to court post-divorce arose for consideration earlier this year in the High Court case of *JC v MC*, unreported, High Court, Abbott J., January 22, 2007. The parties divorced in 2000, following a 21-year marriage and five children. The divorce order was made on the basis of a consent agreement between the parties and included annual maintenance payments of €48,500. Two weeks after the settlement the husband's company interests were sold, increasing significantly the value of his assets. At the hearing, the wife sought a further lump sum order under s.13 and a variation of the existing annual maintenance order under s.22. Interestingly Abbott J. considered the judgment of Keane C.J. in *T v T* [2003] 1 I.L.R.M. 321, but regarded it as very much limited to ample resources cases. In particular Keane C.J.'s suggestion that a new order for maintenance could not be made where one was not granted in the original divorce proceedings was rejected as eliminating what might prove a very important option for couples who might have a great need for such an order in tighter financial circumstances. Thus except in the most financially ample of cases, it appears that it may not be entirely correct to assert that the making of a lump sum order or decision not to make a maintenance order can be a strategic means of barring future applications from the other spouse.

The other key aspect of the judgment of Abbott J. was in relation to the inclusion in the divorce consent order of an agreed full and final settlement clause. In considering such a clause Abbott J. considered the two key issues before the court; the jurisdiction of the court to make *another* lump sum order and the jurisdiction of the court to make or vary a maintenance order. Firstly, Abbott J. considered the jurisdiction of the court to make another lump sum order where a lump sum payment formed part of the ancillary relief orders on granting the decree of divorce. In this regard he was of the view that where the court granting the decree has included as part of the orders made, a full and final settlement clause, it is not then permitted to subsequently make another lump sum order. Thus in this regard, the full and final settlement clause appears to be effective in fulfilling its apparent purpose.

Secondly, with regard to maintenance, the courts have traditionally shown themselves more reluctant to restrict their powers to amend or update this form of financial relief. In the instant case, in respect of maintenance, Abbott J. stated that such a clause should be construed strictly and should only affect or limit the right to order/vary maintenance into the future, where specific alternative orders have been made on granting the divorce, in lieu of maintenance or where it was recognised at the time of granting the decree of divorce, that the right to vary/apply into the future has effectively been waived, expressly or by implication in light of the terms of the consent/order.

Interests of justice

Finally, s.20(5) is perhaps the most vague aspect of s.20 in that it provides that "[t]he court shall not make an order under a provision referred to in s.(1) unless it would be in the interest of justice to do so." The necessity that this requirement be fulfilled serves to add further to the discretion of the judiciary in the division of assets on marital breakdown. Whilst the express inclusion of 12 specific factors in s.20(2), is perhaps an attempt to limit the courts' consideration of influential factors, the decision of the legislature to also include this requirement for justice to be achieved, although admirable in its aim, serves to permit the court to make whatever orders for whatever reason it sees fit. Thus although the specific criteria set out in s.20(2) may have somewhat placed limits on the scope of the discretion of the courts in these matters, s.20(5) ultimately negates such limits.

Ancillary Relief Orders

(1) Maintenance

Section 8 of the 1995 Act and s.13 of the Divorce Act deal with the issue of maintenance and the various forms it can take. For ease and clarity, further discussion of maintenance orders shall refer to the powers under s.13 of the Divorce Act but applies equally to those orders made under the 1995 Act in the context of judicial separation proceedings. The subsections of s.13 of the Divorce Act are identically numbered to those attaching to s.8 of the 1995 Act.

Section 13(1)(a) empowers the court to make a periodical payments order. This is the most common form of maintenance payment, giving rise to a weekly or monthly payment to the dependent spouse and/or dependent children. Section 13(1)(b) provides for the making of a secured periodical payments order which is similar to the periodical payments order but the payment is secured. Section 13(6) provides for the right to make an attachment of earnings order and empowers the court to make such an order in respect of a person to whom earnings fall to be paid. However in deciding to make such an order the court under s.13(6)(b) must give the spouse concerned an opportunity to make representations in relation to the matter and regard must be had by the court to such representations, which may under s.13(6)(c) relate to the question of whether the spouse concerned is a person to whom earnings fall to be paid, and whether he or she would make the payments to which the relevant order relates. Under s.13(1)(c) a lump sum order can be made in respect of the dependent spouse and/or dependent children of the marriage. Section 13(3) provides that an order for the payment of a lump sum can provide for the payment of that lump sum in instalments, to take whatever form the court may specify. All or any of the above orders can be made by the court not only at the time of the granting of the decree of divorce but also at any time thereafter during the lifetime of the respondent or until the applicant spouse dies or remarries (s.13(4)–(6)). In addition under s.13(2) the court may order one spouse to make a payment to the other spouse or any other specified person in respect of any expenses or liabilities reasonably incurred by the other spouse in maintaining herself and any dependent member of the family before the making of the application. Finally a court may order that the maintenance be secured e.g. by the creation of a charge on real property which can be triggered by the spouse if the other spouse is in default.

Maintenance always open to review

It is very well established by case law that the issue of maintenance can never be finalised. In relation to an application for maintenance, it has long been settled that a spouse cannot contract out of maintenance obligations and a spouse retains the right to return to court at any future time to seek further maintenance, despite any covenants to the contrary or orders made by the court. The long-standing position in relation to maintenance as enunciated by Walsh J. in *HD v PD*, unreported, Supreme Court, May 8, 1978 was that "… it is not possible to contract out of the Act by an agreement …". The written consent of the parties in this case, to the application for a divorce *a mensa et thoro*, agreed the payment of the sum of £10,000 to the wife "in full and final settlement of all claims in the petition". However she subsequently initiated proceedings under s.5 of the 1976 Act, seeking a maintenance order for the support of herself and her dependent children. The court entertained her application on the basis that the issue of maintenance can never be conclusively finalised and that a spouse cannot contract out of the right to seek maintenance. Equally in *JH v RH* [1995] 3 Fam. L.J. 96, Barr J. ordered an increase in the maintenance payable by the husband in respect of the wife and children, despite the existence of a separation agreement, which constituted "a full and final settlement of all matters outstanding between them …". In addition, as discussed below, both the 1995 Act (s.18) and the Divorce Act (s.22) also expressly empower either party to return to court at any time after the making of the decree for the variation of an existing maintenance order.

(2) Property adjustment orders

Property adjustment orders, like all other ancillary orders for financial relief can be made by the court on application by one of the parties or on behalf of a dependent member. The division of property under an application for judicial separation is governed by s.9 of the 1995 Act and s.14 of the Divorce Act. Interestingly these two sections mirror each other in terms of content. In addition s.11 of the 1995 Act and s.15 of the Divorce Act relate to the miscellaneous ancillary orders that can be made in respect of the family home. For ease and clarity the discussion of orders in respect of property and the family home will focus on the statutory provisions governing divorce, given the almost identical provisions governing the areas of judicial separation and divorce. Interestingly s.9 of the 1995 Act was amended by s.52(b) of the Divorce Act, thereby causing the two provisions to be identical in content and effect. Where a distinction of legislative treatment arises this will be highlighted.

Section 14 of the Divorce Act empowers the court to make one or more property adjustment orders upon the granting of a decree of divorce:

(a) the transfer by either of the spouses to the other spouse, to any dependent member of the family or to any other specified person for the benefit of such a member of specified property, being property to which the first-mentioned spouse is entitled either in possession or reversion. This is the most commonly exercised order made by the judiciary under s.14 in respect of property.

(b) the settlement to the satisfaction of the court of specified property, being property to which either of the spouses is so entitled as aforesaid, for the benefit of the other spouse and of any dependent member of the family or any or all of those persons. This power can be applied to award a life interest in the family home, by ordering a spouse to place the family home in trust for the benefit of the other spouse and dependent children or equally to establish a trust to be funded by savings or investments of one or both spouses. This power is most often used, particularly in relation to the family home, where it would be inappropriate to transfer it into the sole name of one spouse because of a likely financial imbalance between the parties. Instead a life interest can be awarded to one spouse, resulting for example, in the family home going on reversion to the children of the marriage.

(c) the variation for the benefit of either of the spouses and of any dependent member of the family or of any or all of those persons of any ante-nuptial or post-nuptial settlement (including such a settlement by will or codicil) made on the spouses. Section 14(c) essentially empowers the court to completely reconstruct any ante-nuptial or post-nuptial settlement or agreement made by the spouses, provided it is in favour of either spouse and/or any dependent children. This means that the court can increase, reduce or extinguish a spouse's interest and may even confer an interest on a spouse, previously not provided for. In *FJWT-M v CNRT-M and Trustcorp Services Limited* [2005] 1 I.R. 321, a broad view was taken by the High Court of the concept of a settlement. McKechnie J. stated that what was required to bring a trust within the meaning of this section is that the instrument should confer some financial benefit on one or both spouses as spouses, and with reference to their marital status.

(d) the extinction or reduction of the interest of either of the spouses under any such settlement. In essence, s.14(d) permits the court to reduce or extinguish the share of either spouse under any settlement made between the parties.

The wide range of orders available and the capacity of the courts to make such an order on granting the decree or any time after serves to highlight the extensive powers of the courts. However any right to apply under s.14 of the Divorce Act is terminated by the re-marriage of the applicant. In addition, the operation of s.14 is limited by s.14(7) which prevents an application in relation to a family home in which one spouse is residing with his new spouse.

(3) Family home

When the term property is used in the context of marital breakdown and divorce it is often associated with the family home. The term "family home" as defined by the Supreme Court in *National Irish Bank v Graham* [1995] 2 I.R. 244 is restricted to the precise terms of the Family Home Protection Act 1976:

> "… primarily a dwelling in which a married couple ordinarily reside. The expression comprises, in addition, a dwelling in which a spouse whose protection is in issue ordinarily resides, or if that spouse has left the other spouse, ordinarily resided before so leaving."

Helpfully, s.54(1)(a) of the 1995 Act defines a dwelling as:

> "any building or part of a building occupied as a separate dwelling and includes any garden or other land usually occupied

with the dwelling, being land that is subsidiary and ancillary to it, is required for amenity or convenience and is not being used or developed primarily for commercial purposes, and includes a structure that is not permanently attached to the ground and a vehicle or vessel, whether mobile or not, occupied as a separate dwelling."

Section 10 of the 1995 Act and s.15 of the Divorce Act empower the court to make miscellaneous ancillary orders, and can be applied for by either spouse and/or a person on behalf of a dependent member of the family. One or more of these orders can be made at the time of the granting of the decree of divorce or at any time thereafter, during the lifetime of the other spouse:

- right to occupy the family home for life or other specified period (s.15(1)(a)),
- direct sale of family home subject to conditions, if proper and provide for the disposal of the proceeds between the spouses and any other person having an interest therein (s.15(1)(b)),
- an order under s.36 of the 1995 Act—determination of questions of ownership between spouses in relation to property (s.15(1)(b)),
- an order under ss.5,7, or 9 of the Family Home Protection Act 1976,
- an order under ss.2,3,4 or 5 of the Domestic Violence Act 1996,
- an order for the partition of property under the Partition Act 1868 and the Partition Act 1876, and
- an order under s.11 of the 1964 Act.

In making any of these orders the court shall have regard under s.15(2) of the welfare of the spouses and any dependent children.

As with property adjustment orders under s.14, orders in respect of the family home can be made on granting the decree of divorce or at any time after, during the lifetime of the other spouse. In relation to the accommodation needs of both spouses and any dependent members of the family, the legislature recognised that when making any ancillary order relating to the family home that the court must have regard to the welfare of both spouses and any dependent children and must take into consideration that where a decree of divorce is granted the spouses will no longer reside together. Consequently s.15(2)(b) of the Divorce Act requires the court to ensure that where practicable, proper and secure accommodation is provided for a wholly or mainly dependent spouse and for any dependent members of the family. This section represents a slight change in the attitude of the legislature; s.19 of the 1989 Act, which is now repealed, required the court to have regard to the welfare of the family as a whole; a requirement which is now replaced by the needs of the dependent spouse and dependent children.

Ancillary issues relating to orders for the sale of property

Section 15 of the 1995 Act and s.19 of the Divorce Act are concerned with the ancillary powers of the court where an order for the sale of property has been made. It sets out the number and type of consequential and/or supplementary provisions which such an order can contain. In essence, the court is empowered to include whatever provisions it considers necessary. However without prejudice to these general provisions, s.19(3)(b) contains the following provisions which may be included in an order under s.19:

- a provision specifying the manner of sale and some, or all, of the conditions applying to the sale of the property;
- a provision specifying the person or class of persons to whom the sale of the property is to be offered;
- a provision directing that the sale not have effect until the occurrence of a specified event, or the expiration of a specified period;
- a provision requiring the making of a lump sum payment, or periodical payments, to a specified person or persons from the proceeds of sale; and
- a provision specifying the division of the proceeds of sale between the spouses and any other person(s) having an interest therein, as the court considers appropriate.

Finally, s.15(6) of the Divorce Act represents the legislature's acknowledgement of the existence now or into the future, of one or both parties' new family. It provides that s.19 shall have no application to a family home where, after the granting of a decree of divorce, either of the spouses having remarried ordinarily resides with his or her spouse.

Attitude of the courts to the division of property

Although the typical property adjustment relates to the family home, in many cases the property at issue in a separation/divorce case can include businesses, commercial property, investments and savings. The courts have shown themselves willing to make orders in respect of a business or farm owned by one spouse, or at least award a share of the value of a share in the business to the non-owning spouse. Neither the 1995 Act nor the Divorce Act seeks to limit the discretion exercisable by the court in this area. By declining to specify the assets to be governed by these sections, the legislature has left complete discretion to the courts to make an order in respect of any asset or property of either spouse.

Under s.15 of the 1989 Act, the court could in effect only make a property adjustment order on one occasion and thus the courts' powers have been radically expanded. In the 1997 High Court judicial separation case of *JD v DD* [1997] 3 I.R. 64, McGuinness J. regarded this lifetime right to apply to the court as "the most relevant change from the position under the 1989 Act". Following a 20-year marriage, as the wife had moved out of the family home and was purchasing another property, it was ordered that the family home be transferred into the husband's name. As a result of this the husband was ordered to finance the purchase of the other home for the wife as well as providing for her by way of lump sum order and ongoing annual maintenance payments. Although it was unusual for the family home to be transferred to the husband the particular circumstances made this appropriate and it should be noted that the children were almost all in adulthood. In addition, McGuinness J. acknowledged the wife's remaining right to return to the court in the future, a right which could not be extinguished by the courts.

More typically the family home is transferred into the wife's name either absolutely or until the youngest child reaches the age of majority. This is particularly so where the child or children are of a young age. This approach was discussed by the courts, per O'Dálaigh C.J. in *B v B* [1975] I.R. 54 in circumstances where the parties to the application for a judicial separation had young children. The court made the following observation regarding the importance of the children not only staying together but staying together in the family home:

> "After the separation of the parents there remain two lesser points of unity around which one would wish, if possible, to build: the first of these is the unity of the comradeship of the three children, and the second is the family home where these three children have grown up together."

Despite the limited reported case law available in respect of ancillary relief on marital breakdown it is well-settled that where there are younger children and where it is financially permissible, that the parent with custody should remain in the family home.

In addition to the power to order the sale, transfer etc. of the family home, the broad and unlimited wording of the provisions of ss.9 and 14 as they relate to property adjustment orders give very far-reaching powers to the courts in respect of business assets held by either party to an application for divorce/separation. This has been most evident in recent cases, including the IR£15 million case of *T v T* [2003] 1 I.L.R.M. 321 which represents a significantly different approach from the pre-1995/Divorce Act case of *C(C) v C(J)* [1994] 1 Fam. L.J. 22, where in the High Court, Barr J. declined to make an order in respect of the husband's business premises. He stated that the wife had never had any connection with her husband's business property and therefore was not entitled to any interest therein. Since the enactment of the more extensive provisions regarding ancillary relief in the 1995 Act and the Divorce Act it appears that there is less protection for the assets held by the parties. In *T v T* [2003] 1 I.L.R.M. 321, Fennelly J. considered the provisions of the Divorce Act and was of the view that they suggest:

> "… that any property, whenever acquired, of either spouse and whenever and no matter how acquired is, in principle, available for the purposes provision. Thus, property acquired by inheritance, by chance, or the exclusive labours of one spouse does not necessarily escape the net."

(4) Pension adjustment orders

Introduction

The court is empowered by the very lengthy s.12 of the 1995 Act and s.17 of the Divorce Act to divide the pension held by one or both of the spouses. These detailed legislative provisions are designed primarily to facilitate the division of the pension in order to ensure compliance with the proper provision requirement. This discussion shall refer to the provisions of s.17 of the Divorce Act but applies equally to the mirrored provisions of s.12 of the 1995 Act.

All benefits payable under a pension scheme can be the subject of a pension adjustment order and can be divided into two categories; retirement benefit and contingent benefit. A contingent benefit is a benefit payable to a specified person or persons upon the occurrence of the stated contingency, usually the death of the member spouse while he is still in employment. A retirement benefit refers to all other benefits payable under a pension scheme including the pension paid to a person on retirement or the pension payable to the widow or widower and any dependent member of the family on the death of the member after retirement. An application for a pension adjustment order in respect of both a retirement benefit and a contingent benefit can be made under s.17(2) or s.17(3) by either spouse or by another person on behalf of a dependent member of the family. An order made in respect of a retirement benefit can only be made under s.17(2) in favour of the other spouse or for the benefit of a dependent member of the family, whereas an order made under s.17(3) in respect of a contingent benefit can be made in favour of both. Section 17(23)(a) prevents a spouse who has re-married from seeking a pension adjustment order.

The court can divide a pension by means of earmarking or pension splitting. Earmarking provides that a percentage of the whole or part of a benefit should be paid directly to the other spouse to be invested by him in a pension scheme or alternatively to another person for the benefit of a dependent member of the family. The value of the pension to be earmarked in favour of the non-member spouse is determined by reference to the period of reckonable service to be taken into account and the percentage of retirement benefit accrued to be paid to spouse/other person. This type of payment has been compared with a type of deferred maintenance. The application can be made at any time from the date of such an order until the date of the commencement of the payment of the designated benefit. However pension splitting is not applicable in respect of a contingent benefit and the court can take the entire benefit into account and determine what percentage is payable. Pension splitting means that a percentage of retirement benefits which has been earmarked for the other spouse is valued and is used to provide a separate pension for that spouse. Once such an order is made the recipient spouse can apply to the pension trustees to have the pension split. Such an application can be made at any time up to the payment of the benefit. However pension splitting is not applicable to a pension adjustment order made in respect of a contingent benefit.

Most importantly, s.17(23)(b) requires the court to examine in the first instance the possibility of making proper provision for the applicant spouse on foot of applications for maintenance, property adjustment and financial compensation orders, before considering whether a pension adjustment order should be made. Thus although it may not be appropriate to make a pension adjustment order in every case, the potential to make such an order is likely to influence the division of non-pension assets. For example, in the ample resources case of *BD v JD*, unreported,

High Court, McKechnie J., December 5, 2003 where both parties maintained a claim on the family business, given the significant assets available for distribution the applicant wife was awarded a lump sum of €4million which relieved the court of the need to make a pension adjustment order.

(5) Succession rights

Introduction

The Succession Act 1965 accords special treatment to the relationship of husband and wife. A widow or widower, by virtue of their status as a spouse, is granted an automatic share in the estate of their deceased spouse. If a testator dies leaving a spouse and no children, the spouse is legally entitled to one half of the estate (s.111(1)). If a testator dies leaving a spouse and children, the spouse has a legal right to one-third of the estate (s.111(2)).

Succession rights on judicial separation

Section 17(1) of the 1989 Act allows either spouse to apply to the court for an order extinguishing the share that either spouse would otherwise be entitled to in the estate of the other spouse as a legal right or on intestacy. The provisions of s.17 were adopted for the most part in s.14 of the 1995 Act. In considering the power to extinguish the succession rights of either or both spouses, the 1989 Act required the court to make the order extinguishing the parties' succession rights if the statutory four tier test was applied (s.17(2)(a)–(d)). This test required the court to extinguish the share that the spouse would otherwise be entitled to under the Succession Act where it is satisfied,

(a) that adequate and reasonable provision of a permanent nature has been provided for the spouse whose succession rights are in question,
(b) that provision of a permanent nature is not required to be made for that spouses future security,
(c) that an order has not been made under ss.14, 15 or 16(a), and
(d) that the court is satisfied that if an application was made under ss.14, 15 or 16(a) that an order would not be made by the court.

This four tier test was repealed under the 1995 Act, allowing the court more freedom to make its decision in regard to the extinction of a spouse's succession rights. In contrast to s.17 of the 1989 Act, s.14 of the

1995 Act allows the court to exercise its discretion in the circumstances. Such an order will only be made if it is in the interests of justice to do so, thus it will not usually be made in relation to a dependent spouse if the extinction of that spouse's succession rights would jeopardise his/her future financial security. Conversely alternative circumstances in a case may justify the extinction of these rights. In addition it might also be deemed fair to extinguish these rights if the court has otherwise made adequate financial provision for the spouses, as per the express directions of s.14(a) of the 1995 Act. In practice such an order is nearly always made and alternative forms of security, such as a life assurance policy, are typically put in place.

Succession rights on divorce

The legislature in drafting the Divorce Act did not have to concern itself with including a power to allow the court to extinguish spousal succession rights on the granting of a decree of divorce because at that stage the parties are no longer spouses. Therefore a former spouse can no longer claim entitlement to a legal right share under the terms of the Succession Act. However a former spouse retains the statutory right to apply for a share of the deceased spouse's estate. Such an application can be made by the surviving party under s.18 of the Divorce Act within six months of the death. On foot of such an application, the court under s.18(1) can make such provision for the remaining spouse as it considers appropriate having regard to the rights of any other person having an interest in the matter. In so doing the court must be satisfied that proper provision in the circumstances was not made for the applicant during the lifetime of the deceased spouse under ss.13, 14, 15, 16 or 17. Section 18(2) prohibits the court from making an order under s.18(1) in favour of a spouse who has remarried since the granting of the decree of divorce. If an order is made by the court under s.18 the amount awarded to the applicant (including the value of any property adjustment order and/or lump sum payment) shall not exceed the share in the estate which the applicant would have been legally entitled to under the Succession Act if the marriage had not been dissolved. However this right to apply for a share of the estate of the deceased can be blocked in advance by the court on application by one of the parties (s.18(10)). Section 52(g) of the Divorce Act which inserts s.15(A) of the 1995 Act extends this right to apply to a spouse whose succession rights were extinguished pursuant to an order made under s.14 of the 1995 Act.

Variation of ancillary relief orders

All financial arrangements ordered between the parties on judicial separation and/or divorce are open to review by the court. In addition where the parties have executed a separation agreement and subsequently seek a decree of divorce the court is empowered to review the parties' financial position and make whatever ancillary relief orders necessary to make proper provision for them. However applications for variation of existing orders can be made in their own right, i.e. after divorce or separation orders have been made, under s.18 of the 1995 Act and s.22 of the Divorce Act, as relevant. Thus the courts retain a very wide discretion, even after matters appear finalised between the parties, to vary existing orders, or make further orders in respect of the parties; so-called "second-bite" awards. Existing orders are more likely to be varied where there exists new evidence or there is a change in the circumstances of the parties sufficient to justify a variation. However, it should be noted that although such additional variation is permitted, where the existing orders are recently granted, the court is less likely to significantly change the financial division of assets, unless there was incomplete disclosure or there has been a very significant change in the circumstances of the parties since the existing orders were made.

5. DOMESTIC VIOLENCE

Introduction

The enactment of the Family Law (Protection of Spouses and Children) Act 1976 was the first dedicated statutory recognition of the need for state intervention to protect vulnerable members of the family unit. Prior to this enactment, persons in need of such protection only had recourse to equitable and/or criminal law remedies. The 1976 Act introduced the barring order which removed the violent spouse from the family home for a period of three months. The remedies for abused spouses were enhanced following the enactment of the Family Law (Protection of Spouses and Children) Act 1981 ("the 1981 Act") which extended the life of a barring order to up to one year and introduced the less severe protection order, an interim measure to protect the applicant from the date of application to the date of the hearing of the substantive matter. The shortfalls of the two Acts were evident from the beginning, most particularly because of the very limited category of persons who could seek the relief available. Judicial interpretation of the statutory provisions did not assist the cause of those in need of relief; the Supreme Court in *O'B v O'B* [1984] I.R. 182 restricted greatly the scope of the Act by requiring the presence or threat of physical violence, for an application to be successful. The law was eventually significantly reformed following the enactment of the Domestic Violence Act 1996 ("the 1996 Act"), widening both the categories of persons who could seek relief under the Act and also enhancing the remedies available. Thus as well as strengthening the nature of the remedies available, the 1996 Act has extended legislative protection beyond the inter-spousal relationship.

Domestic Violence Act 1996

The Domestic Violence Act 1996 came into effect in March 1996 and its aims are set out in the long title as follows:

- Make provision for the protection of a spouse and any children or other dependent persons, and persons in other domestic relationships, where their safety or welfare requires such protection arising from the conduct of another person in the domestic relationship,
- Provide for the arrest without warrant in certain circumstances, and

- Provide for the hearing of applications under other legislative enactments related to the domestic relationship.

Remedies available

The nature of the remedies available to those suffering from domestic violence has been greatly enhanced since the three-month barring order was first introduced in 1976. The legislature has recognised the varying levels of violence and danger that may exist and thus has sought to include a variety of remedies to ensure that the court can make an appropriate order in every circumstance. In addition, the availability of remedies of varying severity enhances the constitutionality of legislation that might otherwise be regarded as overly draconian to the respondent and arguably contrary to his right to property or an excessive interference with the family unit. As regards issues other than protection from violence or the threat of violence, s.9 of the 1996 Act recognises that circumstances which might lead to an application under the 1996 Act might often necessitate orders and direction from the court other than under the provisions of the 1996 Act and thus the court is empowered in the course of an application under the 1996 Act, to hear applications under the following statutory enactments:

(a) an order under s.11 of the Guardianship of Infants Act 1964, as amended;
(b) an order under s.5 of the Family Law Maintenance of Spouses and Children Act 1976, as amended;
(c) an order under s.5 of the Family Home Protection Act 1976; and
(d) an order under the Child Care Act 1991.

This important statutory provision which quite sensibly empowers the court to make orders under these somewhat related legislative enactments, without the need for the applicant to institute numerous proceedings, represents recognition of the multi-faceted and complex cases which often come before the courts in this context. Such a related order was made in *JEN v MEN*, unreported, High Court, O'Higgins J., November 9, 2005, a case concerning the ordering of a section 47 report on the welfare of the dependent child in circumstances where in the context of an application for a safety order and a barring order under the 1996 Act, the court made an order relating to custody and access under the 1964 Act.

Barring order

The barring order is the long-standing, and most severe remedy available in the context of domestic violence. A barring order under the 1996 Act and has the effect of removing the respondent from the family home for a stated period and prohibits him from entering the family home for the stated period or until further order of the court (s.3). In addition, if necessary, the court has the power to prohibit the respondent from acting as follows, subject to whatever exceptions and conditions that might be specified by the court:

(a) using or threatening to use violence against the applicant or any dependent person,
(b) molesting or putting in fear the applicant or any dependent person,
(c) attending at or in the vicinity of, or watching or besetting a place where the applicant or any dependent person resides.

A barring order can be made by the court for whatever length of time is appropriate in the circumstances, but will not exceed three years in duration (s.3(8)). However, on application to the court, the barring order can be renewed by order of the court.

Whilst traditionally this remedy could only be sought by a spouse against a spouse, the 1996 Act has enhanced the category of persons who can apply for this relief. Section 3(1) provides that the applicant for a barring order can now include the following persons:

(i) the spouse of the respondent;
(ii) a person who has lived with the respondent as husband or wife for 6 of the 12 months immediately prior to the application;
(iii) a parent of the respondent where the respondent is aged 18 or over and is not dependent upon the parent;
(iv) a person aged 18 or over residing with the respondent in a non-contractual relationship.

In addition, the HSE can apply for a barring order on behalf of any of the above persons (s.6).

Where the applicant under s.3 is a non-spouse, the 1996 Act has included statutory tests as to the applicant's claim on the property where he seeks the sole right of occupancy. Whilst this will be discussed in more detail below, it is important to note that these tests have been necessitated in order to secure the constitutionality of the extended protections under the 1996 Act. Where a non-spouse seeks to remove another from the property where they reside, the requirement that the applicant has an equal or better legal or beneficial interest in the property ensures that the property rights of the respondent are not excessively infringed.

Safety order

A safety order can be ordered by the court under s.2 of the 1996 Act where the court is of the opinion that there are reasonable grounds for believing that the safety or welfare of the applicant or any dependent person so requires. The effect of a safety order is to direct the respondent not to use or threaten to use violence against, molest or put in fear the applicant or dependent persons. The safety order does not remove the respondent from the family home in circumstances where the parties are residing together. If the parties are not residing together, the safety order will order the respondent not to watch or beset the place where the applicant or dependent persons reside. The introduction of this remedy ensured that where a person could not achieve the proofs required to secure a barring order he still had recourse to the courts in circumstances of violence or fear of violence.

The safety order can be made for a period of up to five years and the court can attach any exceptions or conditions to its operation. This is particularly important where access arrangements are in place in respect of any children of the parties, the operation of which might otherwise constitute a breach of the safety order. The breadth of persons who can apply for a safety order under the 1996 Act represents a further welcome development from the restrictive "spouse only" position under the 1976 Act. Section 2(1)(a) provides that the applicant for a safety order can include:

(i) the spouse of the respondent;
(ii) a person who has lived with the respondent as husband or wife for 6 of the 12 months immediately prior to the application;
(iii) a parent of the respondent where the respondent is aged 18 or over and is not dependent upon the parent;
(iv) a person aged 18 or over residing with the respondent in a non-contractual relationship.

In addition the HSE can apply for a safety order on behalf of any of the above persons (s.6).

Interim barring order

The interim barring order was introduced as a remedy by virtue of s.4 of the 1996 Act and acts as a temporary protection measure between the application for a barring order and the full hearing of the case. The court is statutorily empowered to put an interim barring order in place if it is of the opinion that there are reasonable grounds for believing that—

(a) there is an immediate risk of significant harm to the applicant or any dependent person if the order is not made immediately, and
(b) the granting of a protection order would not be sufficient to protect the applicant or any dependent person.

The effect of an interim barring order is to remove the respondent from the family home whilst the interim barring order is in force and to prohibit him from entering such place until such time as the court may specify or until further order of the court (s.4(1)(i)–(ii)).

Notwithstanding the significant impact, albeit short-lived, of an interim barring order upon the rights of the respondent, s.4(3) permits the making of such an order on an ex parte basis where this is regarded by the court as necessary or expedient in the interests of justice. The legislation envisages that such an event would be in "exceptional circumstances" given that the 1996 Act, as originally enacted, permits the making of an interim barring order in the absence of service of the originating document or other notice on the respondent. The constitutionality of this robust power of the courts was considered by the Supreme Court in *DK v Crowley* [2002] 2 I.R. 744 and ultimately lead to a statutory amendment to the court's powers in respect of these orders. The Supreme Court accepted the respondent's challenge to the interim barring order in circumstances where the hearing of the application for a barring order was adjourned on numerous occasions. The respondent claimed that the court's failure to resolve the matter expeditiously constituted a breach of his right to due process and fair procedures. The court accepted these arguments, noting that in enacting the original provisions, the Oireachtas sought to balance the rights of a spouse and child to be protected against physical violence with the constitutional rights of others to due process. Ultimately the court declared the measure to be unconstitutional, stating that the failure of the 1996 Act to prescribe a fixed period of relatively short duration during which an interim barring order made ex parte was to continue in force, deprived the respondent of his constitutional rights to a fair and expedient hearing. The longer-term fallout from this decision was the enactment of the Domestic Violence (Amendment) Act 2002 which addressed the issue directly and amended s.3 of the 1996 Act to require that where an interim barring order is granted on an ex parte basis, the substantive matter must be heard within eight days of the ex parte application. Further a note of the evidence given by the applicant together with a copy of the order, affidavit or information document which grounded the application must be served on the respondent as soon as practicable. The net effect is to rebalance the rights of the parties and ensure that where granted, an ex parte interim barring order has a short lifespan. As a result the respondent is not excessively deprived of his right to be heard nor his right to defend such proceedings.

Protection order

The protection order was first introduced as a statutory remedy under s.3 of the 1981 Act as the interim protective measure for an applicant for the period between the making of an application for a barring order and the hearing of the matter. The protection order has survived the various legislative amendments since and can now be ordered by the court under s.5 of the 1996 Act on application for a barring order or a safety order. Whatever the circumstances in which it is made, the protection order will not survive the determination of the substantive application before the courts. The court will make a protection order under s.5 if it is satisfied, on the making of an application for a barring order or safety order, there are reasonable grounds for believing that the safety or welfare of the applicant or any dependent persons so requires. In making the protection order, the court has the power to direct that the respondent:

(a) shall not use or threaten to use violence against, molest or put in fear the applicant or that dependent person,
(b) and if he or she is residing at a place other than the place where the applicant or that dependent person resides, shall not watch or beset the place where the applicant or that dependent person resides.

In light of *DK v Crowley* [2002] 2 I.R. 744, the constitutionality of the power of the court to grant a protection order was similarly challenged in *Goold v Collins*, unreported, Supreme Court, Hardiman J., July 12, 2004. In judicial review proceedings the applicant sought an order declaring ss.5(1) and 5(2) of the 1996 Act to be invalid having regard to Arts 40.1

and 40.3 of the Constitution. Section 5(1) provides for the making of protection orders and s.5(4) allows such orders to be made in the absence of service of the application upon the respondent. It was claimed by counsel on behalf of the applicant that the fact of the protection order "could tilt the balance in family proceedings before the High Court unfairly against her" with respect to her evidence, her credibility and ultimately could affect judicial decisions regarding the custody and welfare of her children or the nature of ancillary relief orders to be made. These arguments were rejected by Hardiman J. in the Supreme Court and in so doing he highlighted the importance of the 1996 Act as the basis for necessary interim intervention and protectionist measures.

> "... the legislation in respect of domestic violence has been passed by the Oireachtas for a vital social purpose: the protection of spouses and others against lawful assault and, on occasion terrorisation. There is sometimes a necessity for such protection to be provided immediately in an acute situation."

Thus the Supreme Court upheld the validity of the statutory power to make a protection order, even on an ex parte basis and confirmed that the applicant's arguments were not supported in law or in fact. As regards the applicant's attempts to rely upon *DK v Crowley* [2002] 2 I.R. 744, Hardiman J. quite readily distinguished the two cases. He noted that the earlier case had related to an interim barring order and not a protection order, noting that the former, a more severe remedy:

> "... unlike the protection order, has an immediate physical consequence: the Respondent to it must leave his or her home and remain out of it until the order lapses or until further order. The protection order, by contrast, merely enjoins the Respondent to it against the use of violence or threats of violence, which are in any event intrinsically unlawful."

Given that the protection order does not go so far as to remove the respondent from the home, the Supreme Court was satisfied to limit the impact of the *DK v Crowley* decision to interim barring orders.

Who can apply for relief?

Remedies for domestic violence were traditionally only available to spouses. One of the major developments brought about by virtue of the enactment of the 1996 Act was to extend the category of persons who could seek relief under the governing legislation. The statutory right to apply for relief now includes the following:

1) the spouse of the respondent
2) a person who has lived with the respondent as husband or wife for 6 of the 12 months immediately prior to the application
3) a parent of the respondent where the respondent is aged 18 or over and is not dependent upon the parent
4) a person aged 18 or over residing with the respondent in a non-contractual relationship.

The right of these categories of applicants to apply will depend upon the nature of the remedy sought and their capacity to fulfil the statutory proofs required. For example, a person aged 18 or over, residing in a non-contractual relationship is not entitled to apply for a barring order but can seek a safety and/or protection order from the court. In addition the 1996 Act has set out very specific statutory tests to be fulfilled by the applicant where he is not a spouse. Where a cohabiting person seeks a barring order from the court, he must provide evidence that he has lived with the respondent as husband and wife for a period of at least six months in aggregate during the period of nine months immediately prior to the hearing of the application for the barring order (s.3(1)(b)). In addition, and equally in relation to an application by a parent to bar an adult child from the home, there must be evidence that the applicant has a legal or beneficial interest in the property at least equal to that of the respondent(s.3(4)).

Role of the Health Service Executive

Section 6 of the 1996 Act empowers the HSE to apply to the court on behalf of an aggrieved person, for relief under the 1996 Act where it becomes aware of incidents or a threat of harm to the safety or welfare of that person or persons. The HSE is accorded discretion in determining whether to apply for relief under the 1996 Act (s.6(2)) in the following circumstances:

(a) the HSE is aware of an alleged incident or series of incidents which in its opinion puts into doubt the safety or welfare of the aggrieved person,

(b) the HSE has reasonable cause to believe that the aggrieved person has been subjected to molestation, violence, or threatened violence or otherwise put in fear of his safety or welfare,

(c) the HSE is of the opinion that there are reasonable grounds for believing that the aggrieved person would be deterred or prevented as a consequence of molestation, violence or threatened violence by the respondent or fear of the respondent from pursuing an application for a safety order or barring order on his own behalf or on behalf of a dependent person, and

(d) having ascertained as far as is reasonably practicable, the wishes of the aggrieved person, that it is appropriate in all the circumstances to apply on his behalf for a safety order or a barring order.

When hearing an application by the HSE on behalf of an aggrieved person for an order under the 1996 Act, the court is compelled to have regard to any wishes expressed by that aggrieved person and where appropriate, the dependent person(s) (s.6.(3)(a)–(b)).

6. CHILD LAW

Child law

Introduction

As an autonomous individual and citizen of the state the child has historically received little attention from lawmakers. Typically a legal dispute concerning a child involves to some extent, all other family members, and thus historically the Irish legislature and courts have considered the child primarily as a member of the family unit, who is best protected within that family unit, as distinct from focusing upon or asserting his rights as an individual. What is deemed to be in the best interests of the family is regarded to be in the best interests of the child, where the family unit is one based on marriage. Traditionally the Irish courts have been very slow to interfere with parental decisions regarding the upbringing of a child and thus family law has tended to focus on the issue of marital disputes and inter-adult issues arising from the family unit. More recently, however, the child has started to become the focal point of both Irish and international family law.

Under common law rules, no child is legitimate unless his parents are married at the time of his conception or at the time of his birth. The effect of the Status of Children Act 1987 is to equalise the rights of a child vis-à-vis his parents and amend the law relating to his status. Section 3(1) states that "… the relationship between every person and his father and mother (or either of them) shall, unless the contrary intention appears, be determined irrespective of whether his father and mother are or have been married to each other …". The 1987 Act also statutorily provides that a child is now automatically legitimated upon his parents validly marrying regardless of the marital status of the parents at the time of the birth. Henchy J., in *The matter of J, an infant* [1966] I.R. 295, had previously rejected any suggestion that a child, whose parents were married, should be accorded varying constitutional protection depending upon the timing of the marriage. Rather than timing, he highlighted the crucial issue to be the fact of the parent's marriage:

"I find it impossible to distinguish between the constitutional position of a child whose legitimacy stems from the fact that he was born the day after the parents were married, and that of a child whose legitimacy stems from the fact that his parents were married the day after he was born."

However a distinction continues to be drawn between the rights attaching to a child of a marital couple and a child born to unmarried parents. The court in *WO'R v EH* [1996] 2 I.R. 248 has confirmed that the de facto family unit, in this case unmarried parents of a child, is not recognised as deserving of protection under the constitution, as individuals within the unit do have constitutional protection. As regards the rights of children vis-à-vis their parents, no distinction is drawn between marital and non-marital children, for example in relation to succession rights. The child can exercise such rights against both parents irrespective of whether the parents are married.

Welfare of the child

Introduction

Section 11 of the 1964 Act permits any person being a guardian of an infant to apply to the court for its direction on any question affecting the welfare of the infant. The court may give such directions as it sees proper regarding the issues of guardianship, custody and access and may order the father or mother to commence reasonable maintenance payments. The court must as its paramount consideration consider what is in the best interests of the welfare of the child.

Statutory definition

Welfare is defined by s.2 of the 1964 Act as comprising the religious, moral, intellectual, physical and social welfare of an infant. Where proceedings are brought before the court, which relate to the custody, guardianship or general upbringing of an infant, the court is obliged under s.3 of the 1964 Act to regard the welfare of the infant as the first and paramount consideration. In the course of his judgment in *G v An Bord Uchtála* [1980] I.R. 32 at p.76, Walsh J. stated:

> "The word "paramount" by itself is not by any means an indication of exclusivity: no doubt if the Oireachtas had intended the welfare of the child to be the sole consideration it would have said so. The use of the word "paramount" certainly indicates that the welfare of the child is to be the superior or most important consideration, in so far as it can be, having regard to the law of the provisions of the Constitution applicable to any given case."

Thus where there is a conflict between the welfare of the child and other considerations (such as the rights of parents), the welfare of the child should take precedence over all other matters. This principle, that the best interests of the child take preference in all matters concerning the child's welfare, is in line with Ireland's international obligations, in particular with art.3 of the UN Convention on the Rights of the Child 1989 (ratified by Ireland on September 21, 1992).

In the recent case of *M v L* [2007] I.E.S.C. 28 the Supreme Court in assessing the respective claims of the parents and the impact and consequences of their actions, regarded the welfare of the infant as the paramount issue before the court. Denham J. lamented the lack of expert assistance before the court in seeking to assess what might be in the best interests of the welfare of the infant. In this regard, Denham J. affirmed the decision of the High Court to seek a s.47 report, which she stated was necessary and relevant to the fundamental issues of the case.

Judicial pronouncements on the definition of welfare

Religious welfare

Historically any threat to the ongoing religious upbringing of a child would act as a significant obstacle to the arrangements where a particular direction might give rise to such difficulties. Thus, for example, where one party was in a relationship with a person of a different religion to the child, awarding that parent custody would be seen as a threat to the religious welfare of the child. However, the court in *Cullen v Cullen*, unreported, Supreme Court, May 8, 1970 was willing to accept the mother's undertakings that the child would receive proper religious instruction. Therein, despite the mother's religious lapse, the court was assured that the child would continue to be taught religion and would "say his prayers". Perhaps a more balanced approach is now evident in, as in the case of *DFO'S v CA* [1999] I.E.H.C. 147, where the fact that the mother displayed "a commitment to practice" Roman Catholicism, although she was an Anglican, did not represent an obstacle in the custody dispute for her daughter.

Moral welfare

It is no longer an invariable rule of law that a parent who is in an adulterous relationship should be deprived of custody in view of the danger this relationship might pose to the child's moral welfare. In earlier cases the parent who committed adultery was often seen as a source of corruption and as a misguided example for the child. In *JJW v BMW* [1971] 110 I.L.T.R. 49, where the respondent mother had committed adultery, the Supreme Court awarded custody of the three children to the father on the grounds that their moral welfare was more likely to be protected away from the adulterous relationship. Finlay C.J. stated:

> "The fact is that the home which she has to offer to her children is one in which she continues an adulterous relationship with a man who has deserted his own wife and his own two children. A more unhealthy abode for the three children would be difficult to imagine."

However, it has been stated that custody should not be awarded as a prize for good marital behaviour. This more liberal attitude of the court was evidenced in the judgment of Walsh J. in *EK v MK*, unreported, Supreme Court, July 31, 1974: "… custody is awarded not as a mark of approbation or disapprobation of paternal conduct but solely as a judicial determination of where the welfare of the children lies".

Intellectual welfare

The issue of intellectual welfare essentially relates to the intellectual and educational needs of a child. In considering this factor when deciding on the issue of custody, the court must seek to ensure that the result of its decision is that the child is surrounded by intellectual stability and support. This was evidenced in *FN v CO* [2004] 4 I.R. 311 where the court made orders in favour of the maternal grandparents, thereby avoiding any disruption of the children's educational arrangements. Finlay Geoghegan J. specifically noted that an award of custody in favour of the father would significantly and detrimentally impact upon the educational welfare of the children.

Physical welfare

Physical welfare relates to the general physical health and well-being of the child.

Social welfare

The concept of the social welfare of children was best described by Finlay J. in the case of *JC v OC*, unreported, High Court, July 10, 1980 as "their capacity to mix with and enter into and become part of the society in which they will be brought up."

The importance of the examination of these factors as a whole is highlighted by Walsh J. in his judgment in *S v S* [1974] 110 I.L.T.R. 57 which was more recently quoted favourably by McGuinness J. in *CC v PC* [1994] 3 Fam. L.J. 85, who noted that it is necessary for the court to take an overall view:

> "All the ingredients which the Act stipulates are to be considered globally. This is not to be decided by the simple method of totting up the marks which may be awarded under each of the five headings. It is the totality of the picture presented which must be considered ... the word "welfare" must be taken in its widest sense."

In addition however, the welfare of the child is not the only factor to be considered by the court, although it is to be regarded as "the first and paramount consideration" as emphasised by Finlay C.J. in the Supreme Court judgment of *KC and AC v An Bord Uchtála* [1986] 6 I.L.R.M. 65:

> "... it does not seem to me that s.3 of the 1964 Act can be construed as meaning simply that the balance of the welfare as defined in s.2 of the 1964 Act must be the sole criteria for the determination by the court of the issue as to custody of the child."

Other than the issue of the welfare of the child as defined by s.2 of the 1964 Act, the other relevant factors to be considered by the court when determining any issue relating to children can include the following.

Emotional welfare

Section 2 of the 1964 Act does not contain any reference to emotional welfare as an aspect of the welfare of the child but in *DFO'S v CA* [1999] I.E.H.C. 147, McGuinness J. noted that the courts had previously added "emotional welfare" to the statutory list of factors that make up the concept of welfare. In order to have due regard to this aspect of the child's well-being, which she regarded as "a most important aspect of welfare", McGuinness J. was strongly of the view that the parties should resolve their difficulties, and went so far as to suggest, although not order them, to both attend professional counselling. Following on from this,

McGuinness J. asked that future difficulties and disagreements regarding the care of the child be resolved through some form of mediation.

Tender years principle

Finally, the courts have traditionally readily applied the tender years principle in determining the custody of younger children. O'Dálaigh C.J. in his judgment in *B v B* [1975] I.R. 54 stated in reference to the young son of the parties that "in view of his tender age, there can be no doubt that the younger son should continue in the custody of his mother". However the courts do not apply this principle as a rule and in light of varying circumstances is willing to award the father the custody of young children, as in *JJW v BMW* (1971) 110 I.L.T.R. 49. In addition, in light of current attitudes and the changing roles of both fathers and mothers, decisions made now are less likely to adhere to the tender years principle. Fathers are increasingly more available as the principal carer in the family and are becoming more involved in the rearing of their families. This was made most evident by McGuinness J. in *DFO'S v CA* [1999] I.E.H.C. 147 where she discussed the merits of the tender years principle in light of current lifestyles and behaviour:

> "I do not entirely accept the old tender years principle: modern views and practices of parenting show the virtues of shared parenting and the older principles too often meant the automatic granting of custody to the mother virtually to the exclusion of the father."

In all the circumstances McGuinness J. made an order of joint custody despite the fact that the child was merely four years old. Similarly, in *GT v KAO* [2007] I.E.S.C. 55; unreported, High Court, September 10, 2007, McKechnie J. suggests that perhaps there should be a greater societal recognition of the father who, albeit not married to the mother of his child, "from the moment of birth, nurtures, protects and safeguards his child; sometimes to a standard which all too frequently married fathers fail to live up to" (para.50).

Child as rights holder

Although it is clear that the Constitution provides express protection and rights for the family, for the most part, the rights of the individual members of the family do not receive any specific attention in its provisions. Article 41 protects the family as a social unit, thus any rights, enumerated or otherwise attach to the family as a collective. However, in *Re Article 26 and the Adoption Bill 1987* [1989] I.R. 656, the Supreme Court, per Finlay C.J., rejected the submission:

> "… that the nature of the family as a unit group possessing inalienable and imprescriptible rights, makes it constitutionally impermissible for a statute to restore to any member of an individual family constitutional rights of which he has been deprived by a method which disturbs or alters the constitution of that family if that method is necessary to achieve that purpose."

Thus whilst the family unit is protected specifically by Art.41.1.1, this does not prevent the vindication of the rights of individual members of the family. The judgment delivered by the Supreme Court in this Article 26 judgment referred to the child's "natural and imprescriptible rights", noting further that such rights are referred to in Arts 40, 41, 42, 43 and 44. Ultimately, given the objective of the impugned Adoption Bill, the court confirmed that despite the inalienable and imprescriptible rights of the family under Art.41.1.1, the State can vindicate and restore the personal rights of a member of a family by altering the constitution of that family if necessary. In *WO'R v EH* [1996] 2 I.R. 248, Barrington J. interpreted the meaning of Art.42 which refers to the "natural and imprescriptible rights of the child" to include references to the "inalienable rights and duties of parents and to the imprescriptible rights of the child". He further commented that "… the rights of the child are clearly predominant …" in any conflict or dispute.

Notwithstanding the near absence of a direct reference to the child in the provisions of the Constitution, the courts have shown themselves willing to establish many implied or unenumerated rights of the child. The matter was given attention by the Supreme Court in *G v An Bord Uchtála* [1980] I.R. 32 where O'Higgins C.J. recognised the child's right to bodily integrity as well as the right to an opportunity to be reared with due regard to religious, moral, intellectual and physical welfare. He emphasised the child's rights as incorporating the right:

> "… to be fed and to live, to be reared and educated and to have the opportunity of working and realising his or her full personality and dignity as a human being. These rights of the child … must equally be protected and vindicated by the State."

Walsh J. referred to the child's right:

"... to rest and recreation, to the practice of religion, and to follow his or her conscience ... the right to maintain ones life at a proper human standard in matters of food, clothing and habitation ...The child's natural right to life and all that flows from that right are independent of any right of the parent as such."

In his dissenting judgment in *North Western Health Board v HW and CW* [2001] 3 I.R. 622, Keane C.J. recognised an important relevant principle, previously identified by Ellis J. in *PW v AW*, unreported, High Court, April 21, 1980:

"In my opinion the inalienable and imprescriptible rights of the family under Article 41 of the Constitution attach to each member of the family including the children. Therefore in my view the only way the 'inalienable and imprescriptible' and 'natural and 'imprescriptible' rights of the child can be protected is by the courts treating the welfare of the child as the paramount consideration in all disputes as to custody, including disputes between a parent and a stranger. I take the view also that the child has the personal right to have its welfare regarded as the paramount consideration in any such dispute as to its custody under Article 40.3 and that this right of the infant can additionally arise from 'the Christian and democratic nature of the State'."

In the same case Hardiman J. placed great emphasis on what he regards as the misapprehension regarding the position of children in the Constitution, noting that it would be "quite untrue to say that the Constitution puts the rights of parents first and the those of children second". What is apparent from the judgments in this recent adoption/ custody case is the paramount importance of the married family, and the legal presumption that the welfare of the child is best served within that unit.

Child's right to be heard

Section 25 of the 1964 Act as inserted by s.11 of the Children Act 1997 requires the court in any proceedings to which s.3 applies:

"as it thinks appropriate and practicable having regard to the age and level of understanding of the child take into account the wishes of the child on the matter."

Similarly, art.12 of the UN Convention on the Rights of the Child 1989 provides as follows:

> Every child has the right to express views freely in all matters and to have their views given due weight in accordance with the age and maturity.
> The child shall in particular be provided the opportunity to be heard in any judicial and administrative proceedings affecting the child, either directly, or through a representative or appropriate body, in a manner consistent with the procedural rules of natural law.

It is also intended by the legislature that the wishes of the child can, where appropriate, be expressed through the appointment of a guardian *ad litem* who will represent the child independently in matters that affect the welfare of the child. Section 28 of the 1964 Act, as amended by the Children Act 1997 aims to provide for the appointment of a guardian *ad litem* where it is necessary in the interests of the child. However this section has not yet been commenced. Section 27(1) of the 1997 Act permits the court to proceed with the hearing of applications under ss.6A, 11 or 11B of the 1964 Act in the absence of the child, although where a child requests to be present, s.27(2) obliges the court to grant the request of the child, unless it appears that, having regard to the age of the child or the nature of the proceedings, it would not be in the best interests of the child to do so. In practice where the court deems it necessary and appropriate to consider the express wishes of the child, the court will invite the child to give evidence. This can be done in the courtroom or the judge might bring the child into his chambers to allow him or her to speak more freely. Finlay Geoghegan J. considered the effect of s.25 of the 1964 Act in *FN v CO* [2004] 4 I.R. 311, concerning an application for custody by the maternal grandparents of two girls whose mother had died. The girls, aged 14 and 12 at the time of the hearing were regarded by the court as being of an age and maturity to make it appropriate for their wishes to be taken into account. However Finlay Geoghegan J. emphasised that s.25 does not oblige the court to follow the wishes of the child when making the relevant decision. She further noted that Art.40.3 of the Constitution entitles children to be heard in a custodial hearing, referring to "the natural and imprescriptible rights of the child referred to in Art.42.5 of the Constitution". Finlay Geoghegan J. regarded the inclusion of s.25 as recognition by the Oireachtas of a child's right to be heard under Art.40.3 of the Constitution. The enactment of the European Convention on Human Rights Act 2003 now requires the court to endeavour to ascertain the wishes of any child aged seven or older, regarding his welfare.

Proposed Constitutional Amendment

Whilst most family law legislative enactments state that the welfare of the child is the paramount consideration for the court, the Irish Constitution has long represented an obstacle for the adequate protection of children's rights. Given that the children, at best, are regarded as rights holders arising from their membership of the family, rather than from any independently existing rights of the child, the call for Constitutional reform has been long-standing. The Twenty-Eighth Amendment of the Constitution Bill 2007 (S.I. No.14 of 2007) was published in February 2007 in response to intense calls for reform of children's rights. In its press release, the Government claimed that as drafted, the Constitutional amendment would provide a framework within which Irish law would continue to develop to enshrine the highest possible standards of protection for children. The proposed amendment seeks to replace the existing Art.42.5 and to insert a new Art.42A as follows:

"Article 42(A)
1. The State acknowledges and affirms the natural and impre-scriptible rights of all children.
2. 1. In exceptional cases, where the parents of any child for physical or moral reasons fail in their duty towards such child, the State as guardian of the common good, by appro-priate means shall endeavour to supply the place of the parents, but always with due regard for the natural and imprescriptible rights of the child.
    2. Provision may be made by law for the adoption of a child where the parents have failed for such a period of time as may be prescribed by law in their duty towards the child, and where the best interests of the child so require.
    3. Provision may be made by law for the voluntary placement for adoption and the adoption of any child.

4. Provision may be made by law that in proceedings before any court concerning the adoption, guardianship or custody of, or access to, any child, the court shall endeavour to secure the best interests of the child.

5. 1. Provision may be made by law for the collection and exchange of information relating to the endangerment, sexual exploitation or sexual abuse, or risk thereof, of children, or other persons of such a class or classes as may be prescribed by law.

   2. No provision in this Constitution invalidates any law providing for offences of absolute or strict liability committed against or in connection with a child under 18 years of age.

   3. The provisions of this section of this Article do not, in any way, limit the powers of the Oireachtas to provide by law for other offences of absolute or strict liability."

The impact of such an amendment to the Constitution, if accepted by the people has been strongly criticised. It has been suggested that it has failed to enhance the position or rights of the child under Irish law and that the Government has lost a valuable opportunity to grant express protection for children's rights (Kilkelly U. and O'Mahony C., "The Proposed Children's Rights Amendment: Running to Stand Still" (2007) 2 I.J.F.L. 19).

Guardianship, custody and access

Introduction

Whereas being awarded sole custodian rights to the child gives rise to responsibility for the everyday care of the child, a parent who is awarded guardianship rights without custodial rights is entitled to be consulted in respect of the major decisions relating to the child's life and lifestyle. Time spent with the child by the non-custodian parent will be governed by any access agreement between the parties or any access orders, by consent or otherwise.

On marital breakdown the issues of custody and access will always arise where there are dependent children. Guardianship is less likely to arise as an issue as the married parents are already joint guardians of the child or children; s.10(2) of the Divorce Act ensures that this status is not affected by the granting of a decree of divorce. In essence the right of custody means that the child will reside primarily with that custodial parent although Irish law now recognises the concept of joint custody where parents are separated. As long as a parent retains their guardianship status they remain involved in the fundamental care and upbringing of the child. The issues of custody and access can never be finally resolved and are always open to and subject to further applications for variation by either parent (s.12 of the 1964 Act). The court will consider what arrangements are in the best interests of the child, as required by the provisions of s.3 of the 1964 Act which states that the welfare of the child is the first and paramount consideration. The 1964 Act has been regarded as "a statutory statement of what is inherent in the Constitution" insofar as it "reinforces the common law position that the court is entrusted with the responsibility of the child's welfare." In the context of state intervention in the family, and the placing of a child in the care of the state, O'Flaherty J. in *Southern Health Board v C*, unreported, Supreme Court, March 11, 1996 stated that the role of the court is to "undertake an investigation of what is in the best interests of the child: whether to be placed with the father or the Board." When balancing conflicting rights, O'Flaherty J. prioritised the rights of the child as the "primary obligation" and focus of the court, followed by a need for the rights of the father to be safeguarded. However it was quite definitely stated that "the child's welfare must always be of far graver concern to the Court".

Guardianship

Guardianship means the rights and duties of parents in respect of the upbringing of their children. It encompasses the duty to maintain and properly care for the child and refers to the decisions that must be made during the child's lifetime which relate to the general lifestyle and development of the child. Being a guardian requires a person to partake in the important decisions in a child's life, e.g. education, religion, general rearing etc.

Who can be a guardian?

The natural mother of a child is automatically a guardian of the child, under s.6(4) of the 1964 Act the unmarried mother is the sole guardian and her automatic right to custody is set out in s.10(2) of that Act. Whether the father of a child is an automatic guardian depends upon his relationship with the mother. The married mother and father of a child are the most common guardians and they are so entitled by virtue of s.6(1) of the 1964 Act. However for the father to have guardianship status the parties must be married at the time of the birth of the child. Alternatively he can acquire guardianship status if the parties marry at some time after the birth of the child. Other methods for appointment as guardian of a child include an application under s.6A of the 1964 Act, a statutory declaration signed by both parents agreeing to the appointment of the father as guardian, and thirdly, the appointment as testamentary guardian, effective upon the death of the mother. These methods by which the natural father can be appointed guardian of his child will be considered further in the chapter on the non-marital family.

Custody

Custodial rights of parents

Custody has been judicially defined as the right of a parent to exercise physical care and control in respect of the upbringing of their child on a day-to-day basis (per Denham J., *WO'R v EH* [1996] 2 I.R. 248). More recently, McGuinness J. in the Supreme Court regarded custody as encompassing the "crucial decisions regarding the child's health and education and the carrying into effect of those decisions" (*NAHB, WH and PH v An Bord Uchtála, PO'D* [2002] I.E.S.C. 73). McGuinness J. cited s.10 of the 1964 Act and Art.40.3 of the Constitution in support of the mother's position as sole guardian and custodian of a non-marital child. The married parents of a child are automatically joint guardians and custodians of their child by virtue of the Constitution. However, s.18(1) of the 1964 Act provides that the court may declare a parent guilty of misconduct to be a parent unfit to have the custody of the children of the marriage and thus in the event of the death of the other parent that parent would not be entitled as of right to the custody of the children. In addition s.18(2) provides that a clause in a separation agreement providing that one of the parents of an infant gives up the custody or control of the child shall not invalidate the agreement. Historically such a clause would have been deemed contrary to public policy and therefore enforceable or could have caused the invalidation of the agreement as a whole.

The parental right to custody, whether relating to one parent or both is never absolute. Notwithstanding the stated statutory right under the 1964 Act of an unmarried mother to the sole custody of her child, the Supreme Court in *NAHB, WH and PH v An Bord Uchtála, PO'D* [2002] I.E.S.C. 73 has confirmed that this right to custody "is by no means absolute". Although the particular rights of the mother "derive from the fact of motherhood and from nature itself", the State has an underlying

Constitutional obligation to intervene where necessary to vindicate the rights of the child. In this regard, McGuinness J. quotes favourably from the judgment of O'Higgins C.J. in *G v An Bord Uchtála* [1980] I.R. 32, who stated that:

> "... these rights of the mother in relation to her child are neither inalienable nor imprescriptible ... [t]hey can be alienated or transferred in whole or in part and either subject to conditions or absolutely, or they can be lost by the mother if her conduct towards the child amounts to an abandonment or an abdication of her rights and duties."

Such limitation or deprivation of the custodial rights can now also be imposed upon the married parents of a child or children, by virtue of both adoption and child care legislation which seeks to protect the vulnerable minor child/children in a family environment. Finally, it is important to note the "interlocutory" nature of custody orders, as stated by the Supreme Court (*B v B* [1975] I.R. 54). Given the ever-changing and evolving nature of the needs and welfare of a child, the courts have emphasised the importance of their capacity to revisit custodial arrangements and alter them where necessary.

Joint custody

Joint custody is an option open to parents and the courts when the issues relating to the children are being determined. Section 9 of the Children Act 1997 amends s.11 of the 1964 Act by inserting a statutory right in appropriate cases, to award custody of a child to a father and mother jointly. However, the practicalities of life are such that most often children will reside with one parent whilst exercising access with the other parent. In the High Court case of *EP v CP*, unreported, High Court, November 27, 1998, McGuinness J. in awarding sole custody to the applicant mother in the context of separation proceedings, and whilst noting that joint custody is currently recommended, emphasised that it cannot work satisfactorily for the children if there is a high level of conflict between the parents. She further noted that when couples cannot work together sensibly and happily in the interests of the children, an order for joint custody is not suitable. Thus it appeared from this judgment that only where the spouses have an amicable relationship should the court consider a joint custody order. However, more recently, McGuinness J. in *DFO'S v CA* [1999] I.E.H.C. 147 in a situation of "bitterness and resentment" was of the view that if the parties were to accept the joint responsibility of caring for their daughter and promoting her welfare, it might "encourage them to put their antagonisms behind them". In the course of her judgment McGuinness J. noted that:

> "As a general rule where there is deep hostility between the parents I am very reluctant to make an order granting joint custody, due to the probable inability of the parents to co-operate in caring for the child." (at 25)

The courts now appear to prefer to make orders for joint custody and have stressed that this does not afford each party rights to equal time with the child but rather ensures that each parent has rights and corresponding obligations to the child.

Access

The parent who does not obtain custody of a child but remains a guardian is entitled to apply for access to the child. In fact a parent who is refused guardianship status remains entitled to apply for custody, or more likely access, subject to the direction of the court (s.11(4) of the 1964 Act). The courts have repeatedly emphasised, that where one party is awarded custody, there is no loss of guardianship rights accruing to the non-custodian guardian. It has been noted that a parent "so deprived of custody can continue to exercise the rights of a guardian ... [and] ... must be consulted on all matters affecting the "welfare" of the child ..." (Walsh J. in *B v B* [1975] I.R. 54). The court will consider an application for access on the basis that the best interests of the child is the paramount consideration. Where there is a conflict between what is in the best interests of the applicant parent and the child, the rights of the child should take precedence. As with a custody order, an access order is never a final order, it is always open to either parent to apply to the court to vary the access order if this is in the interests of the child. It is extremely unusual for a court to refuse a parent access with his/her child. *AMacB v AGMacB*, unreported, High Court, June 6, 1984 exemplifies the strong judicial tendency in favour of granting access. Notwithstanding that evidence was presented that the children feared him, Barron J. was of the view that it was "essential that the children know that they have a father and ... that their father is able to take the place of a father in their lives" (at 13). The court will try to accommodate any case where access would be inappropriate by making an order of supervised access. In *O'D v O'D* [1994] 3 Fam. L.J. 81, for instance, the High Court granted supervised access to the father where there was a reasonable suspicion that he might have sexually abused his child.

Rights of non-parents

The Children Act 1997 introduced on a statutory footing, the right of relatives to apply for access to a child. Section 9 of the aforementioned Act which inserted s.11B into the 1964 Act followed the High Court ruling in *D v D* [1993] 1 Fam. L.J. 34 where Carroll J. stated that the right of the child to access extends beyond the right of access to his parents, to that of access to grandparents and the extended family of the child. Section 9 provides that a relative of the child or a person who has acted in loco parentis to a child can apply for access to that child. Any order made by the court following such an application can be made subject to whatever terms and conditions are deemed appropriate by the court. However an application can not be made under s.9(1) without the applicant first applying for, and being granted by the court leave to make an application under s.9(2). This gives rise to difficulties given the tensions that will invariably exist where a grandparent or other relative is required to seek the assistance of the court. In deciding to grant the leave to apply the court must have regard to all the circumstances as a whole and must in particular consider the following, as set out under s.9(3):

(a) the applicant's connection with the child,
(b) the risk, if any, of the application disrupting the child's life to the extent that the child would be harmed by it,
(c) the wishes of the child's guardians.

Given the likelihood of conflict between the applicant and the child's guardians it will be difficult for the applicant to convince the court that the leave should be granted. The High Court case of *FN v CO* [2004] 4 I.R. 311 involved a custody dispute regarding two teenage sisters, between the maternal grandparents and the widowed, separated father. The girls had resided with their grandparents, firstly in Belgium and later in Ireland, for eight years prior to the hearing. Although previous proceedings before the Belgian courts had dealt with various issues including responsibility for the day-to-day care and custody of the girls, the proceedings before the High Court were initiated by the grandparents who sought a number of orders, including guardianship and sole custody of the girls. Although in such circumstances the court noted that there exists a presumption that the children's welfare is best served in the custody of their father, this presumption is rebuttable, and was on the facts before the court, rebutted by the applicants. Given the particular circumstances before the court, this was regarded as an exceptional case, which required the grandparents to be awarded custody of the girls. Interestingly, Finlay Geoghegan J. chose to comment on the "deep antagonism evidenced in the course of these proceedings" which she suggested might cause concern for the welfare of the children in the future. She thus regarded it necessary to take the unusual step of relying upon s.11 of the 1964 Act to direct that a third party intermediary mechanism be utilised, to permit the father and maternal grandparents to communicate civilly in relation to issues pertaining to the children.

Guardianship, custody and access on marital breakdown

Undoubtedly the complexities and hostility often faced by the court in addressing issues of access and custody are further complicated by ongoing matrimonial difficulties. The Supreme Court has noted the added difficulties in such circumstances, recognising the occasional need, for a parent to be declared unfit for custody. O'Dálaigh C.J. has indicated a marked reluctance for the court to reach such a conclusion, noting that "the welfare of the children will rarely be advanced by a verdict of condemnation of one or other of the parents".

In general the courts prefer to keep siblings together, ideally in the family home. The courts favour continuity and stability for the children even where the behaviour of the custodial parent is an issue. O'Dálaigh C.J. in the aforementioned case *B v B* [1975] I.R. 54 emphasised the significance of the "unity of the children" and the need for this to be maintained, ideally in his view, in the family home in which they have grown up. This he regards as "the other point of unity". He regards the family home as "a stabilising influence and should help minimise the upset which must necessarily have been suffered". The comradeship that O'Dálaigh C.J. speaks of in this earlier case is repeated by Finlay Geoghegan J. in *FN v CO* [2004] 4 I.R. 311. In this regard she mentions the "strong sibling bond" between the two sisters, which necessitates that they remain together.

In *RC v IS* [2003] 4 I.R. 431 the court considered parental rights post separation. It was noted that the non-custodian parent and guardian of a child remains entitled to be consulted on matters of importance, as distinct from day-to-day matters, particularly those issues relating to the physical and social welfare of the child. This was deemed to include decisions as to whether the child should reside in the State and whether the child should remain in the educational system of the State, or be educated in a different state. The applicant, the non-custodian guardian of the child was regarded by Finlay Geoghegan J. as having "rights of custody" within the meaning of art.5 of the Hague Convention on the Civil Aspects of International Child Abduction ("the Hague Convention"), which she regarded as the right jointly with the mother, to determine, inter alia, the child's place of residence.

7. NON-MARITAL FAMILY

Introduction

The family, although referred to and protected by the Constitution, is not expressly defined by any article of the Constitution. The text of Art.41 recognises the family as the "natural primary and fundamental unit group of society" and as "a moral institution possessing certain inalienable and imprescriptible rights" which are "antecedent and superior to all positive law". However, in evaluating the breadth of the protections available, the courts have confined the concept of the family to the family based on marriage, based on the specific reference to the marital family, and the obligation on the State to protect it; Art.41.3.1 contains a pledge by the State to "guard with special care the institution of Marriage, on which the Family is founded, and to protect it against attack". Consequently, a marriage that is not valid according to Irish civil law will not be recognised as a family unit for the purposes of constitutional protection and rights.

In delivering the judgment of the Supreme Court in *State (Nicholau) v An Bord Uchtála and the AG* [1966] I.R. 567, Walsh J. drew very definite lines of delineation between the marital and non-marital family:

> "While it is quite true that un-married persons co-habiting together and the children of their union may often be referred to as a family and have many, if not all, of the outward appearances of a family, and may indeed for the purposes of a particular law be regarded as such, nevertheless so far as Article 41 is concerned the guarantees therein contained are confined to families based on marriage." (at 643–644)

Rights of the child

Historically the courts were very slow to interfere with the upbringing of a child and traditionally family law focused on the issue of marital disputes and the relationship between the parents of the child. More recently however, the child has become the focal point of both Irish and international family law. The family based on marriage enjoys particular protections and rights under Art.41 of the Constitution and for the most part, the State cannot interfere in the decisions made by the family in

97

respect of the formation and/or upbringing of the children. Notwithstanding this, the Irish legislature and courts will not ignore the interests or welfare of a child who may be in danger. The welfare of the child is a matter of both private and public concern. Thus Art.42 refers not only to the rights of parents but also to their obligations in respect of their children. In exceptional cases where parents have failed in their duty towards their children the State is obliged under Art.42.5 to intervene with a view to defending the welfare of the children. Ultimately it is for the parents to have responsibility and care for the children, with the State intervening in the event of the child being in a position of danger.

At common law no child is legitimate unless his parents are married at the time of his conception or at the time of his birth. The Children Act 1987 provides that a child is now automatically legitimated upon his parents validly marrying regardless of the marital status of the parents at the time of the birth. There is no difference between the constitutional position of the legitimate or legitimated child, as was stated by Henchy J. in *Re J* [1966] I.R. 295 and confirmed by the Supreme Court in *KC and AC v An Bord Uchtála* [1985] I.R. 375.

However the court in *WO'R v EH and An Bord Uchtála* [1996] 2 I.R. 248 has confirmed that the de facto family, in this case unmarried parents of a child, is not recognised as deserving of protection under the constitution. The court also stated that fathers' rights are only to be taken into account when deciding issues such as guardianship.

Rights of the unmarried parents

Section 3(1) of the Children Act 1987 provides that:

> "the relationship between every person and his father and mother
> (or either of them) shall ... be determined irrespective of whether
> his father and mother are or have been married to each other, and
> all other relationships shall be determined accordingly."

One aspect of Irish family law that continues to expressly distinguish between the rights of the conflicting parties is that of guardianship/ custody law. Whether the father of a child is an automatic guardian depends upon his relationship with the mother. The natural mother of a child who at the time of the birth is not married to the father of the child is, by virtue of the Constitution and the subsequent statutory enactments, the sole guardian and custodian of that child. Section 6(4) of the 1964 Act provides that the unmarried mother is the sole guardian and her automatic right to custody is set out in s.10(2). As distinct from this, the father of a child born in circumstances where he is not married to the natural mother of the child is in a very weak legal position. He has no automatic entitlement to a legal relationship with that child, rather his only right is to apply to the courts for guardianship/custody/access rights, or alternatively to agree such rights with the mother.

Attaining guardianship status

Section 6(1) of the 1964 Act states simply that the father and mother of an infant shall be guardians of the infant jointly. However, this apparently wide definition is quickly limited by the definition of "father" in s.2 of the Act, which excludes the natural unmarried father of a child. Section 11 of the 1964 Act permits any person being a guardian of an infant to apply to the court for its direction on any question affecting the welfare of the infant. The court may give such directions as it sees proper regarding the issues of custody and access and may order the father or mother to commence reasonable maintenance payments. The court must as its paramount consideration consider what is in the best interest of the child.

The natural father of the child who is not married to the mother of the child can apply to the court under s.6A of the 1964 Act (as inserted by s.12 of the Status of Children Act 1987) to be appointed a guardian of the child. However the easiest way for the unmarried natural father to become a joint guardian of the child is by obtaining the mother's agreement and co-operation. Section 4 of the Children Act 1997 inserts a new s.2(4) in the 1964 Act which enables a father to be appointed a guardian of the child with the mother's agreement provided they enter into a statutory declaration, declaring that they are the father and mother of the child, that they are not married to each other, that they agree to the appointment of the father as a guardian of the child and they have entered into arrangements regarding the custody of and access to the child. The form of the statutory declaration is set out in the Guardianship of Children (Statutory Declaration) Regulations 1998 (S.I. No.5 of 1998). It is not necessary to cite the relevant custody and/or access arrangements on the declaration. As a result this declaration removes the need for the parties to attend the District Court in order for the father to be appointed a guardian. However where there is no agreement between the parties, the right to apply to court to be appointed a guardian remains a right of the father. A guardian appointed under the 1964 Act shall be entitled to make an application for custody of the child and shall be entitled to take proceedings for the restoration of his/her custody of the child against any person who wrongfully takes away or detains the child. Alternatively/in addition he can apply for access to the child.

Case law concerning the non-marital family

Several cases have come before the Supreme Court which have dealt with the right of a natural unmarried father to be appointed as guardian of his child. In *JK v VW* [1990] 2 I.R. 437, a case stated by Barron J. from the High Court to the Supreme Court, it was held that s.6A of the 1964 Act gives a natural father the right to apply to be appointed a guardian but does not give him the right to be a guardian, nor does it equate his position in law with the position of a father married to the mother of his child. Finlay C.J. in the course of his judgment stated:

"The discretion vested in the Court on the making of such an application must be exercised regarding the welfare of the infant as the first and paramount consideration. The blood link between the infant and the father and the possibility for the infant to have the benefit of the guardianship by and the society of its father is one of the many factors which may be viewed by the court as relevant to its welfare."

In *WO'R v EH and An Bord Uchtála* [1996] 2 I.R. 248, although most of the issues involved related directly to the matter of adoption, one question stated by the Circuit Court judge related to the character and extent of the rights of interest or concern of a natural father: when they arise in an application for guardianship and whether such matters within the sole discretion of the trial judge? In relation to the father's right to be appointed a guardian of the child, Hamilton C.J. discussed the decision in the earlier case of *JK v VW* [1990] 2 I.R. 437 where in the High Court Barron J. had stated that he interpreted s.6A as stating that the rights of the father should not be denied by considerations of the welfare of the child alone, but only where there are good reasons for doing so. The matter was ultimately resolved by way of case stated to the Supreme Court, wherein the limitation of the rights of the father to a right to apply, was confirmed by Finlay C.J.:

"Section 6A gives a right to the natural father to apply to be appointed guardian. It does not give him a right to be a guardian, and it does not equate his position vis-à-vis the infant as a matter of law with the position of a father who is married to the mother of the infant."

This view was adopted by Hamilton C.J. when he confirmed that s.6A creates merely a right to apply for guardianship. The varying nature of the rights and duties of the unmarried father of a child was highlighted later in that case by the Supreme Court, given the multitude of circumstances that could come before the courts in such cases. It was held by the Supreme Court that although the basic issue for the trial judge is the welfare of the children, consideration must be given to all relevant factors. The blood link between the natural father and the children will be one of the many factors for the judge to consider, and the weight it will be given will depend on the circumstances as a whole. Thus, in the absence of other factors beneficial to the children and in the presence of factors negative to the children's welfare, where the blood link is the only link between the father and the children, it is of small weight and can not be the determining factor. But where the children are born as a result of a stable and established relationship and nurtured at the commencement of life by their father and mother in a de facto family as opposed to a constitutional family, then the natural father on application to the court under s.6(A) of the 1964 Act has extensive rights of interest and concern. However they are always subordinate to the paramount concern of the court which is the welfare of the child. This long standing view of the father's mere right to apply has been questioned recently by the High Court. In *M v L* [2007] I.E.S.C. 28, discussed in detail below, McKechnie J. emphasised the importance of the relationship between the parent and child when assessing the rights of the unmarried father. He was particularly critical of the view that a father might simply have a right to apply, fearing that such a restrictive approach would impact negatively upon the dynamic of the father/child relationship. Ultimately, though, the views of McKechnie J. have lost weight given that this issue was not addressed by the Supreme Court on appeal.

The case of *NAHB, WH and PH v An Bord Uchtála* [2002] 4 I.R. 252 centred on a custody dispute between the long-term foster parents and the natural unmarried mother of the child. The applicant foster parents sought an order under s.3(1) of the Adoption Act 1988, dispensing with the consent of the natural unmarried mother. In applying a purposive interpretation to the legislation, the court regarded the actions of the mother as a real and objective abandonment of her rights as a parent, ultimately dismissing her appeal of the adoption order. The natural mother, as notice party to the proceedings, sought to rely upon her automatic statutorily recognised rights under s.10 of the 1964 Act as natural guardian and custodian of the child, to seek the return of her child. This "right" to custody was disputed by McGuinness J., who regarded it as by no means absolute, citing both statutory and constitutional bases for exceptions to such a claim. In this regard, McGuinness J. noted that given the notice party's status as an unmarried mother, her rights in relation to her child were neither inalienable nor imprescriptible.

The difficult adoption case of *N v Health Service Executive, and An Bord Uchtála* [2006] 4 I.R. 374 considered the elevated rights of the natural parents given that they had married since agreeing to place the child for adoption. In light of their change of status as a couple and as now *married* parents of the child, McGuinness J. regarded them as a "constitutional family" with all the resultant "concomitant rights and presumptions". McGuinness J. and the Supreme Court as a whole were quick to emphasise that the dispute was not to be adjudicated on the basis of the best interests of the child but rather on the lawfulness of the foster parents' custody. However she did highlight the heavy burden placed on the applicant foster parents to establish the "compelling reasons that her welfare could not be achieved in the custody of her natural parents".

In *M v L* [2007] I.E.S.C. 28 the rights of a non-marital father to involvement in his child's life was again considered by the Supreme Court. The factual context was slightly different; the natural father and mother had by arrangement agreed that the child would be conceived by artificial insemination and when born, would be in the custodial care of the natural mother and her same-sex partner. In a written agreement between the parties, it was stated that the child would know that the respondent was his father and the respondent would be welcome to visit the child at times mutually convenient to all. Following difficulties with that arrangement and ultimately the appellant's decision to move with the child to Australia for 12 months, the respondent sought the direction of the court under the 1964 Act, the Child Abduction and Enforcement of Orders Act 1991 and art.8 of the European Convention of Human Rights to prevent the removal of the child from the State and to secure his position as a legal guardian and custodian of the child. He secured these orders in the High Court and the matter was appealed to the Supreme Court.

In considering the rights of the natural mother, Abbott J. in the High Court noted that notwithstanding the written contract between the parties, the mother was the "sole guardian of the child and has her natural constitutional rights and is entitled to custody of the child to the exclusion of all persons". Despite this fundamental position of law, Denham J. in the Supreme Court recognised the right of the father to apply to be appointed guardian and regarded this as a fair question to be tried in the circumstances. Ultimately however, Denham J. admitted to being guided by "the paramount importance of the welfare of the infant, by the young age of the infant, by the fact that a year is a long time in the life of a developing infant, and by the injustice that would be done to the infant if the applicant is ultimately successful in his application". Interestingly "justice" for the child was not presumed to automatically be best served in the sole care and custody of the natural mother. However as this hearing was to adjudicate on an interlocutory application only, the matter of the status of the natural father has yet to be resolved. Fennelly J. did regard it necessary to distinguish between the respondent in this case and the natural father in the earlier case of *JK v VW* [1990] 2 I.R. 437, given that the father in that case had had a serious relationship with the mother, they had lived together and had planned the birth of the infant as a couple. Whether the court will use the unusual relationship between the parents in *M v L* [2007] I.E.S.C. 28 to seek to limit the rights of the respondent at the hearing of the substantive issue is yet to be seen.

Most recently in *GT and KAO v the Attorney General* [2007] I.E.H.C. 326 the High Court has delivered a statement of the law relating to fathers' rights, with a strong emphasis on family rights under art.8 of the European Convention on Human Rights. McKechnie J. ruled that the rights of an unmarried father were breached after his former partner removed his children from Ireland to England without his consent. At the time of the removal, the father did not have guardianship status in respect of the children. It was noted that the parties had spent the three years of their relationship "living like man and wife and as part of a de facto family unit". Interestingly McKechnie J. was of the view that had the parties been married to each other the resolution of the dispute "would be entirely straightforward". Thus he was of the view that the matter would be determined by a decision as to the "rights, if any, an unmarried father has in respect of his children in this jurisdiction". Numerous sets of proceedings co-existed in this dispute, including an application under the 1964 Act for the resolution of the three issues of guardianship, custody and access and co-existing proceedings under the Hague Convention. Proceedings were also issued in the High Court of England and Wales under the Hague Convention on the Civil Aspects of International Child Abduction and Council Regulation 2201/2003.

Under the Hague Convention proceedings a number of key issues were considered by the court. In order to decide if the removal was "wrongful" the court set out those questions to be determined, as follows:

(a) the extent of the relationship between the applicant and the respondent and in particular the role which the former has played in the lives of his children,

(b) the place of the children's habitual residence in January 2007 and, if Ireland, for how long thereafter did that remain the position,

(c) whether rights of custody vested in any person, institution or other body within the law of the State of habitual residence immediately before the children's removal or retention,

(d) whether those rights were in fact being exercised or would have been exercised but for the children's removal or retention, and

(e) whether there was breach of such rights.

McKechnie J. placed great emphasis on both the relationship between the parties and the relationship between the applicant and the children. Although the exact extent of the applicant's involvement with the children was disputed between the parties, it was accepted that the applicant performed duties and undertook parental responsibilities for them. Further evidence was accepted that most frequently he catered for the needs of the children in the mornings and was responsible for taking them to school/ crèche as necessary. He was regarded as being "very much involved with his children in all aspects of their development and upbringing". Ultimately, McKechnie J. stated that he was bound by the Supreme Court decision of *HI v MG* [1999] 2 I.L.R.M. 1 which had refused to recognise inchoate rights of custody under the Hague Convention but he confirmed that such qualified rights of custody existed for the applicant for the purposes of Brussels Regulation II bis. McKechnie J. was anxious to emphasise that he was not creating a new rule of law, but rather such an assessment must occur on a case by case basis. Ultimately the court ruled that:

(1) the children's removal from the state was a wrongful removal within the meaning of art.2 of Council Regulation No. 2201/2003/EC as constituting a breach of the rights of custody of the applicant.

(2) The retention of the children outside the jurisdiction constituted a breach of the rights of custody vested in the court, and accordingly was wrongful within the meaning of art.2 of Council Regulation No. 2201/2003/EC and art.3 of the Hague Convention.

However the court could not rule in favour of the father's attempt to have those rights of custody vested in him, given the reluctance of McKechnie J. to disturb the meaning of the "rights of custody" under Irish law.

McKechnie J. helpfully stated the current domestic position, summarised as follows:

1. (a) A family based on the institution of marriage is the only family entity recognised by and entitled to the protection of Art.41 and Art.42 of the Constitution. No other family unit, howsoever established, functioning or stable, is within these provisions.

   (b) It follows that neither the natural mother or the natural father have any rights to their non-marital child under either of these Articles.

2. An unmarried mother has however, certain natural rights inter alia to the custody and care of her child under Art.40.3 of the Constitution.

3. An unmarried natural father has no such natural rights to his child which attract the protection of Art.40.3 of the Constitution or any other article.

4. A non-marital child enjoys the same constitutional rights as children born within marriage. Discrimination between such children born within marriage was abolished by the Status of Children Act 1987, harmonising Irish law with the European Convention on Human Rights.

5. The mother and father of a child, who are married to each other, are the joint guardians of their child. On the death of either, the survivor, if any, together with any other guardian appointed by the deceased, shall be the guardians of such a child. These and all other statutory rights are in addition to the constitutional rights above identified.

6. Both male and female adopters, under an adoption order, are treated as having exactly the same statutory rights as those above mentioned.

7. Every such guardian shall be the guardian of both the person and the estate of the child unless the deed of appointment or will or order of the court provide otherwise. Subject to any such restriction, every guardian shall be entitled, as against all other persons save for his joint or co-guardian, to the custody of his child.

8. An unmarried mother of a child, whilst living is entitled to the sole guardianship of her child unless there is in existence a s.6A order, or the mother and father have made a statutory declaration conferring upon the latter, the status of guardian, or any other person has been so appointed under the 1964 Act.

9. Under s.6A of the 1964 Act, as inserted by s.12 of the 1987 Act, the court, on application by the natural father, may appoint him to be the guardian of the child.

10. Any guardian may apply to the court for its directions on any question affecting the welfare of the child. "Welfare" includes the religious, moral, intellectual, physical and social welfare of the child. Section 11(4) of the 1964 Act, as inserted by s.13 of the 1987 Act provides a natural unmarried father who is not a guardian may use this section to seek directions with regard to the custody and/or rights of access to his child.

11. Section 3 of the 1964 Act states that in any proceedings before the court, touching upon inter alia the custody, guardianship, upbringing of a child, the welfare of that child shall be the first and paramount consideration.

12. For the purposes of art.3 of the Hague Convention, an unmarried father, by reason only of that status, does not have any 'rights of custody' in respect of his child. 'Inchoate Rights' are not recognised in this jurisdiction.

Ultimately McKechnie J. emphasised the importance of the relationship between parent and child when assessing the rights, if any, which may arise. In particular he queried the accuracy of the view that an unmarried father might only have the right to apply to claim rights in respect of his children. Rather, any rights that a father might have "are founded upon, and evolve and develop by reason of, his relationship with his child, and if it exists, with the child's mother". McKechnie J. regarded the court's role as simply to declare the fact of these rights, such rights in his view, being "alive and present" before any court hearing. Ultimately he was critical of this notion of a father's mere "right to apply" and regarded it as negatively impacting upon the dynamic of relationships in such circumstances. What is clear from his judgment is the attention focused upon the particular facts of the case and the nature of the relationship between all the parties involved. The High Court appears to be moving away from generalised statements as regards familial and relationship rights and rather appears anxious to examine individual relationships and assess the nature and extent of the rights accruing, by virtue of the fact and character of the relationships. Ultimately the removal of the children was declared unlawful by McKechnie J. This view was reiterated by the Supreme Court on appeal by the children's mother (*T v O* [2007] I.E.S.C. 55). Murray C.J. for the Supreme Court confirmed the father's right to initiate these proceedings as the natural, unmarried father of the children. Ultimately the Supreme Court regarded the applicant mother's wrongful removal of the children as depriving the court of the rights of custody attributed to it.

Succession rights in the context of the non-marital family

Since June 14, 1988, children born outside marriage have the same succession rights as those born within a marital union. Section 28 of the Status of Children Act 1987 amended s.3 of the Succession Act 1965 to provide that all parent/child relationships are to be regarded equally irrespective of the marital status of the parents of the child. This statutory provision overturned the decision of the court in *O'B v S* [1984] I.R. 316 which held that a non-marital child could have no succession rights to his father's estate. In addition, as with any child, a child born outside the marital union can bring an application under s.117 of the Succession Act if he is not satisfied that he was properly provided for by his parent during the lifetime of that parent, irrespective of whether the will was drafted before or after June 14, 1988. In relation to the succession rights of a cohabitee, as the law currently stands, he has none, but provision can be made for a cohabitee in a will by way of bequest. However such a bequest cannot interfere with the legal right share of a spouse.

Rights of cohabitees under Irish law

Currently, an unmarried cohabitee has no legal right or entitlement to maintenance for himself from his non-spousal partner, whether co-habiting or otherwise. In respect of any children of the union, main-tenance can always be sought pursuant to s.5 of the 1976 Act, as amended. An application for child maintenance can also be initiated under s.11(2)(b) of the 1964 Act. Neither is a cohabitee protected by the terms of the Family Home Protection Act 1976. The terms of the 1995 Act and the Divorce Act do not apply unless the parties are engaged. Thus a cohabitee has no right to apply for ancillary relief in respect of a property where she may reside with her partner unless she has a legal claim in the property. The only avenue open to a non-engaged couple is to seek relief under general equitable principles, typically premised upon the existence of a trust or proceedings under the Partition Acts 1868–1876. In *Ennis v Butterly* [1996] I.R. 426, the Irish courts considered the position of a cohabiting couple who had entered into a written agreement to marry in the future and to cohabit as man and wife until they were legally entitled to marry. The plaintiff argued that on the basis of this agreement, she had discontinued her business and worked as a full-time housewife for the benefit of the respondent and thus sought damages for breach of contract, negligent misrepresentation and fraudulent misrepresentation. In striking out the applicant's claim in contract, Kelly J. stated that s.2(2) of the Family Law Act 1981, in abolishing the action for breach of promise of marriage, was fatal to any claim deriving from the breach of the defendant of an agreement to marry her. Any agreement which purported to replicate the marital relationship was contrary to public policy and unconstitutional, given that it might have the effect of undermining the institution of marriage. However Kelly J. did permit the issue of damages arising from misrepresentation to go to hearing given that the action of the plaintiff in abandoning her business might have been induced as a result of misrepresentations on the part of the defendant and insofar as that claim was advanced as an alleged tortious wrong it must be permitted to proceed to trial as it could not be said that the plaintiff's claim in this regard would definitively fail.

Finally, following lengthy delay, the Heads of the Civil Partnership Bill were published in June 2008, to provide an outline of the general scheme of the proposed Civil Partnership Bill. According to the Government, the aim of the Bill will be to establish a statutory mechanism for registration of same-sex partnerships with a statutory statement of the duties and responsibilities of registered partners, to include the consequences of the dissolution such partnerships. In addition, Pt 7 of the Bill seeks to bring greater certainty to the legality and enforceability of cohabitation agreement. It appears that the Bill, when published will allow for the type of inter parte contract that was in dispute in *Ennis v Butterly* [1996] I.R. 426. The Bill, however, will not extend to the provision of a right to marry to same-sex couples.

8. ADOPTION LAW

The purpose of the adoption process is to facilitate and regularise the procedure whereby a child is permanently placed in the care of one or more adults on the basis of a parent-child relationship. This can be necessitated following the death of a parent or parents, through failure of parental duty, or can be elected by the parent or parents of the child. The role of adoption law is to create a structure whereby the nature and extent of legal duties and obligations can be clearly established to ensure that minimum confusion or controversy arises. The effect of the making of an adoption order is to place the adoptive parents in the legal position as if they were the natural parents of the child being adopted. Section 24 of the Adoption Act 1952 provides that upon an adoption order being made—

(a) the child shall be considered with regard to the rights and duties of parents and children in relation to each other as the child of the adopter or adopters born to him, her or them in lawful wedlock;

(b) the mother or guardian shall lose all parental rights and be freed from all parental duties with respect to the child.

Adoption in Ireland provides for the permanent transfer of parental rights and duties from the birth parents to the adoptive parents. The regulation of the adoption process under Irish law has long been affected by a number of principles and presumptions. Until recently only the child of a non-married couple could be considered for adoption, given the protection of the married family under Irish Constitutional family law, and the underlying presumption that a child's interests are always best served within the confines of the natural family. The central issue for consideration in most contentious cases before the courts has related to the consent of one or both natural parents, and whether it was validly given or whether it can be withdrawn at a late stage in the process. The issue of the need for the consent of the natural unmarried father has also received significant legislative and judicial attention and has generated contentious debate.

History of adoption legislation

Adoption Act 1952

The principal Act governing adoption in Ireland is the Adoption Act 1952 ("the 1952 Act"). When enacted, this was a groundbreaking piece of legislation insofar as it introduced statutorily regulated adoption of children to Ireland. Prior to this development, such an arrangement would have been privately organised and often finalised by way of private adoption deed. However given the lack of statutory recognition or regulation of such arrangements, their enforceability was always in doubt. Unsurprisingly such agreements were regarded as contrary to public order, given that their purpose was to invalidate the rights of the natural parents of a child. Part II of the 1952 Act is entitled "Adoption Orders" and deals with key issues surrounding the adoption process, including the requirements for the making of a valid adoption order, establishes An Bord Uchtála (The Adoption Board), and identifies those children who can be adopted as well as those who can be considered as applicants in the adoption process. In addition this Part outlines the legal requirements for a valid consent to the adoption of a child. Part III of the 1952 Act deals with the legal implications arising upon the making of an adoption order, dealing inter alia with parental rights and duties, property and succession rights and the impact of the marriage of the natural parents subsequent to the making of the adoption order. Finally Pt IV regulates the registration of Adoption Societies and outlines the requirement for the involvement of such a society in the adoption process.

An Bord Uchtála

Section 8 of the 1952 Act establishes the Adoption Board, known as An Bord Uchtála, which is empowered to make an order for the adoption of a child on the successful application of a person or persons. The Board currently consists of a Chairman and eight ordinary members. The Board is empowered to make an adoption order in respect of a child, upon the application of a person desiring to adopt that child. Walsh J. on behalf of the Supreme Court in *G v An Bord Uchtála* [1980] I.R. 52 regarded the Adoption Board as, in effect "a ratifying agency and a safeguard". The role of the Board, in his view, is to ensure that each adoption is "made in accordance with the Acts of the Oireachtas and that the prospective adopters are suitable". In essence he noted that the Board:

> "... is simply concerned with what ... is the administrative function of seeing that the steps being taken are not contrary to the adoption legislation, are not inimical to the welfare of the child, and that everybody concerned has had a full opportunity of considering the matter carefully. It is quite clear that the Board

was not invested with any power to settle or decide any question as to the existence of a right or obligation or duty."

Another key function of the Adoption Board under the 1952 Act is the creation and maintenance of an Adoption Societies Register. The Adoption Board can under s.36(1), include in that register, any body of persons which seeks registration where adequate information is furnished to the Board regarding the status and purpose of that body. Section 36(2) prohibits the Board from registering any body of persons unless it is satisfied that the purpose of the body is the promotion of charitable, benevolent or philanthropic objects, charitable or otherwise and that the body is competent to discharge its statutory obligations as a registered adoption society. The importance of a successful registration as an adoption society is highlighted by s.34 of the Act which provides that it is unlawful for any body of persons to make any arrangements for the adoption of a child unless that body is a registered adoption society.

Adoption process and procedure

Although the principal Act governing adoption in Ireland is the 1952 Act, it has subsequently been amended by the Adoption Acts of 1964, 1974, 1976, 1988, 1991 and 1998. The adoption process is also affected by other, related enactments, most recently by the provisions of the Child Care (Amendment) Act 2007.

Who can be adopted and who can adopt?

Introduction

The primary aim of the 1952 Act is to provide a statutory framework for the lawful adoption of a child. Under that Act (as amended) the adoption can lawfully take place of a child which is defined as any person under 18 years of age. The 1952 Act, in its original form required that a child be "illegitimate or an orphan" to permit him to be adopted which reflected at that time, an unwillingness on the part of the State to intervene in the marital family irrespective of the circumstances that the child might find himself in. There existed an unwavering presumption and expectation that the welfare and best interests of the child were always best served within the confines of the marital family. Notwithstanding this presumption, s.29 of the Act provides that where a valid adoption order has been made, the subsequent remarriage of the natural parents of the adopted child can not serve to invalidate the order made. Undoubtedly this proviso is essential in order to ensure some level of stability and certainty for all parties involved. In the case of *The Matter of J, an infant* [1966] I.R. 295, Henchy and Teevan JJ. awarded custody to the now married natural parents of a child, whose adoption order had earlier been quashed by the High Court because of the invalidity of the mother's consent. Henchy J. stated that in deciding this case, the rights of the applicant natural parents could only be met by awarding them the custody of the child and concluded that the natural parents "must have custody".

The adoption of marital children

Notwithstanding this recognition by Henchy J. of the constitutional presumption that the welfare of a child is best served within his marital family of origin, the quasi rule that marital children are better placed within their own family can and does give rise to injustices, as marital status alone is no guarantee of a family's functional success. The issue was given consideration by the Review Committee on Adoption Services and outlined in their 1984 Report of the Review Committee on Adoption Services. The Committee recommended that all children should be eligible for adoption irrespective of the marital status of their parents:

> "In our view, it is wrong that any child deprived by circumstances of a family life should have to spend his childhood in care when, but for a legal obstacle, he could have the permanency and security of an adoptive home ... we are strongly of the view that a legal process is required which would permit the dispensation of agreement to placement for adoption in appropriate cases".

The Adoption Act 1988

The Adoption Act 1988 did not greatly overhaul the adoption process in Ireland but did extend the scope of children who could be subject to an adoption order to include children born within a marital union where, in exceptional circumstances, the parents for physical or moral reasons have failed in their duty towards their children. Denham J. has observed the Adoption Act 1988 to be a "child-centred" piece of legislation, which "seeks in rare, exceptional cases" to place children for adoption, where it is in their interests to do so (*SHB v An Bord Uchtála, MO'D and MO'D* [2000] 1 I.R. 165). Section 2 of the Act empowers the HSE, on application by the person(s) seeking to adopt a child born within a marital unit, to make a declaration of its willingness to make an adoption order given the suitability of the parties, subject to a successful application under s.3(1) to the High Court. The second tier of the process involves that application to the High Court and in the absence of the permission of the High Court, or on appeal the Supreme Court, the adoption cannot proceed. Section 3 sets out the proofs that must be satisfied before a non-consensual adoption order can be made in respect of a child, including a marital child:

(I)   (A) for a continuous period of not less than 12 months immediately preceding the time of the making of the application, the parents of the child to whom the declaration under section 2(1) relates, for physical or moral reasons, have failed in their duty towards the child,

      (B) it is likely that such failure will continue without interruption until the child attains the age of 18 years,

      (C) such failure constitutes an abandonment on the part of the parents of all parental rights, whether under the Constitution or otherwise, with respect to the child, and

      (D) by reason of such failure, the State, as guardian of the common good, should supply the place of the parents,

(II)   that the child–

      (A) at the time of the making of the application, is in the custody of and has a home with the applicants, and

      (B) for a continuous period of not less than twelve months immediately preceding that time, has been in the custody of and has a home with the applicants,

(III) that the adoption of the child by the applicants is an appropriate means by which to supply the place of the parents.

Where these proofs are satisfied, the court may, if it is in the best interest of the child to do so, having had due regard for the rights of the persons concerned including the rights of the child, make an order authorising the board to make an adoption order in relation to the child in favour of the applicants.

The 1988 Act broadens the scope of the adoption process, expanding it to act as a means of protecting all children in need of assistance, including marital children. Such intervention in the marital family was defended by the legislature because of the need to ensure that whatever familial arrangements are in place, the court must have the capacity to vindicate the rights of every child under the Constitution. To maintain an absolute statutory bar on the adoption of marital children would have prevented the intervention of the court even in the most extreme cases. Unsurprisingly, this legislative change has not seen the floodgates opening in respect of the adoption of marital children; rather the non-consensual adoption of a child, including a child born in wedlock has been permitted in exceptional and very restricted circumstances.

Predictably, the constitutionality of the Act was considered by the Supreme Court when the Bill was referred by President Hillery. Finlay C.J., as reported in *The matter of Article 26 and the Adoption (No. 2) Bill 1987* [1989] I.R. 656 upheld the validity of the Bill and stated that the rights of the family guaranteed in Arts 41 and 42 of the Constitution could not operate to deny the personal rights of a particular member of that family. He rejected the contention that the nature of the married family as a unit group made it constitutionally impermissible to identify and restore the rights of an individual member of that family where such an action would disturb or alter the constitution of that family. Regarding the form that the parental failure may take, Finlay C.J. confirmed that the State is entitled to intervene wherever necessary in order to "supply the parental duty to cater for the personal rights of the child", both enumerated and unenumerated and the State's obligations to the child and entitlement to intervene in the family unit was not limited to circumstances where the parents had failed to provide education for their child or children. Regarding the level of failure required on the part of the parents, Finlay C.J. stated that the most important element of this concept of failure is that it must be "total in character". Further, a failure due to "externally originating circumstances such as poverty" would not amount to a failure for these purposes. Denham J. has considered the meaning of term "abandonment" as utilised by the legislature, noting that in this context it has "a special legal meaning" which was not equivalent to deserting or forsaking a child (*Southern Health Board v An Bord Uchtála* [2000] 1 I.R. 165). Relying upon these views, the Supreme Court has more recently noted that the test of abandonment is an objective one and does not require an intention to abandon (*NAHB, WH and PH v An Bord Uchtála and PO'D* [2002] 4 I.R. 252).

The added statutory requirements that the court be satisfied that the parental failure is likely to continue without interruption until the child attains the age of 18 years further serves to emphasise the extent of the proof of physical and moral failure required by the legislature and in turn the courts, before an adoption order can be made.

Adoption of marital children—case law

The Adoption Act 1988 has set out detailed requirements as regards the circumstances where a court might properly consider the making of an adoption order in respect of a child born to a married couple. It is clear that the legislature chose to limit the discretion of the courts to the adjudication of the extent of the abandonment in question and otherwise set out prescribed behavioural tests to be fulfilled to the satisfaction of the court. The term abandonment, which is at the centre of the legislative test has received significant judicial attention and has been considered with reference to the other major legislative proof contained in the 1988 Act that a parent must, for physical or moral reasons, have failed in their duty towards the child in question. The provisions of the 1988 Act were first judicially considered in its original Bill format arising from the Article 26 Presidential referral to the Supreme Court. The central issue for consideration was whether in permitting the adoption of marital children, the 1987 Adoption Bill constituted an unjust attack on the family and was thus regnant to the provision of the Constitution that sought to protect the institution of the family.

In considering the legislative test, Finlay C.J. on behalf of the Supreme Court highlighted its multi-faceted nature, noting that s.3 provides "a series of matters which seriatim must be established to the satisfaction of the court". He insisted that they are framed in a "much more stringent form of being absolutely essential proofs requiring separately to be established". Rather than viewing the tests collectively, Finlay C.J. emphasised the individual nature of the tests to be fulfilled and stressed that failure to fulfil any one of the legislative proofs would absolutely prohibit the making of a s.3 order by the court, irrespective of the strength of the evidence before the court as regards the desirability of an order being made from the point of view of the best interests of the child. Thus whilst certain behaviour might provide evidence to support arguments in respect of each of the tests, the statutory standard required for each of the tests had to be separately fulfilled to the satisfaction of the court. One of the first cases to consider the issue of parental failure and abandonment is not of great assistance as a precedent, given the dearth of information regarding the circumstances which lead to the child's placement in a Delhi orphanage. The Irish Supreme Court granted the adoption order in *Eastern Health Board, TM and AM v An Bord Uchtála* [1994] 3 I.R. 207 involving an Indian child who had been abandoned by unknown parents shortly after her birth. Although the central issue before the court was whether the provisions of the 1952 Act, as amended, could apply to the adoption of an "alien" child, Finlay C.J., having considered s.3 at length, accepted that where the only evidence before the court is that the child was "completely and totally abandoned within days of its birth", this had to be regarded as sufficiently comprehensive evidence to satisfy the provisions of the Act.

The multi faceted statutory test was considered by Lardner J. in the High Court, whose decision was later confirmed by the Supreme Court (*Western Health Board, HB and MB v An Bord Uchtála, TR and GR* [1995] 2 I.R. 178), where he ultimately had refused to make an order in respect of a child of married parents. Following marital difficulties and an extra-marital affair on the part of the wife GR, the husband TR left the family home. In February 1988 they had sexual intercourse without her consent. Infant M was born in November 1988, and although GR did not believe TR to be the child's father, she named him on the birth certificate. GR placed M with foster parents and in May 1989 M was placed for adoption as an extra-marital child. However tests showed that TR was the father of M and he sought to prevent her adoption. In considering the father's attempts to prevent the adoption order being made, whilst Lardner J. was satisfied as regards the first two proofs required, i.e. that that had been a failure in parental duty towards the child in the previous 12 months and that failure was likely to continue until the child attains 18 years, he was not satisfied that the evidence before the court was such as to prove abandonment of all parental rights on the part of the father. Thus the application was refused as in light of the father's conduct; his delay and procrastination, his expressed reluctance to give up the child and his expressed claim to recover her, Lardner J. was unable to conclude under s.3(1)(I)(C) that the proper inference was that his conduct amounted to a total and final abandonment of his rights as a parent within the meaning of s.3.

The Supreme Court, in confirming the decision of the High Court agreed that fulfilling the first two aspects of the statutory test could not automatically represent sufficient evidence of an abandonment of all parental rights. Evidence of the father's behaviour and attitude towards the child, including a refusal to sign the declaration that he was not the natural father, his express desire to see the child and have her returned from the adoptive parents and his issuing of a summons claiming custody of the child served to defeat the contention that he had abandoned his parental rights in respect of the child.

The Supreme Court again considered the workings of these legislative proofs in *Re F.O'D an Infant: SHB v An Bord Uchtála, M.O'D and*

M.O'D [2000] 1 I.R. 165. The infant, F.O'D was the 11th child to a deprived travelling family. In December 1987, a social worker visited the campsite where the family caravan was then located and discovered F.O'D tied by a piece of string to a window inside the caravan. His hands and feet were blue with the cold and he had a severe nappy rash. He was later diagnosed as being on the verge of pneumonia. He was placed with foster parents, Mr and Mrs C until August 1989 when he was returned to his natural parents pursuant to a District Court order. In December 1989 he was admitted to hospital with non-accidental multiple fracture and bruises, as well as strap marks to his body. He was placed once more with Mr and Mrs C and his parents made no access requests until the adoption application was made. The foster parents made an application to the High Court for a s.3(1) order having been considered by the Health Board and deemed suitable to adopt F.O'D. In the High Court Costello J. authorised the making of the adoption order on the basis that the parents had failed in their duty towards F.O'D and was satisfied that the numerous s.3 requirements had been proven to the court. The parents appealed the decision to the Supreme Court, claiming that the criteria laid down by s.3(1) of the Adoption Act 1988 had not been fulfilled. The five judges of the Supreme Court were in agreement in their support of the decision of Costello J. Denham J. in delivering the main judgment of the court, regarded it necessary and appropriate to highlight the extent of the parents "substantial cruelty … and neglect" of the boy. She noted that the neglect was both physical and psychological, leaving him with an ongoing post-traumatic stress disorder. In considering the provisions of the Adoption Act 1988, and in particular the different aspects of s.3, it is clear that the court regarded them as representing distinct proofs to be met, each to be considered with reference to the circumstances before the court. With regard to the first step; whether the parents have, for physical or moral reasons, failed in their duty towards the child, it was noted that this test "has a high threshold" and requires the presence of strong evidence to establish a failure of duty by parents towards the child. Whether such failure will continue until the child reaches majority is determinable on the facts before the court, and in the instant case Denham J. was satisfied that this second requirement was certainly fulfilled. The third and final step, whether the parental failure constitutes abandonment, it was stated that the image of the desertion or forsaking of a child is not the notion of abandonment to be applied in this context. Rather Denham J. stated that the word 'abandonment' is used as a special legal term. Importantly, the section does not require that there be an intention to abandon. The legal term 'abandon' can be used also where, by their actions, parents have failed in their duty. Notwithstanding that the parents in this case did not abandon F.O'D in the sense of deserting him physically in a place; the courts were not precluded from rejecting their appeal.

The issue of parental abandonment of duties was given considerable consideration by both the High Court and Supreme Court in *Northern Area Health Board, WH and PH v An Bord Uchtála, and P O'D* [2002] 4 I.R. 252. The child, J., at the time of the proceedings was almost 14 years of age. Her mother came from an extremely deprived family and was, as a child, for a time placed in voluntary care of the local health board. When J. was born, the mother was 21 years of age. After the birth she was totally unresponsive to the needs of her baby. On account of her inability to care for her baby, J. was admitted to voluntary care with the local health board when she was six weeks old. She was placed with short-term foster parents, but because she was a very difficult baby, this was not successful and she was then placed in a group home for children. In July 1989, the second and third applicants, Mr and Mrs H, were approved as long-term foster parents for J., and in August 1989, J. was placed in their care. She remained in their care continuously since that time. In June 1990, when she was 18 months old, J. was diagnosed as suffering from cerebral palsy with right hemiplegia. Over the years Mr and Mrs H provided a happy and secure family life for J. In September 1997, the birth mother was diagnosed as suffering from chronic schizo-affective psychosis in addition to her mild mental handicap. The High Court heard evidence that this condition was permanent and could only be controlled by anti-psychotic and sedative drugs. Mr and Mrs H had long been anxious to adopt J., who had become in a real sense a member of their family. The birth mother however, was unwilling to agree to this, despite assurances that she would continue to be able to visit J. and despite the fact that she was perfectly satisfied to leave J. in their permanent long-term foster care. Regarding the issue of the notice party's abandonment of J., the principles set out in the decision of *Southern Health Board v An Bord Uchtála* [2000] 1 I.R. 165, were specifically approved. In all the circumstances Herbert J. concluded that the notice party had abandoned the custody and care of her daughter to the applicants. She had left and would continue to leave to them crucial decisions regarding the child's health and education and the carrying into effect of those decisions. This situation amounted in a real and objective sense to abandonment of her rights as a parent. Furthermore, the infrequent visits by her to her daughter, largely initiated by others, were not inconsistent with the reality of her abandonment of her position as a parent.

In an important clarification, the Supreme Court held that opposition to adoption by a parent in itself did not contradict the fact of abandonment. The test of abandonment was an objective one and an intention to abandon was not required. A mere statement by a parent or parents that they wished to abandon a child would equally not necessarily constitute proof in any particular case of the fact of abandonment. To provide otherwise would be to defeat the child-centred purpose of the 1998 Act by a parental statement of opposition/abandonment.

Consent

The issue of consent in the context of adoption was first statutorily regulated by ss.14 and 15 of the 1952 Act. The valid placement of a child for adoption involves a two-stage process of consent. The process whereby a parent agrees to put her child forward for adoption and places the child with the adoption agency or prospective adopters is regarded as the initial consent, or consent to place. Finlay P. preferred to regard this aspect of the process as an agreement rather than consent (*S v Eastern Health Board*, unreported, High Court, Finlay P., February 1979). Subsequent to this, the consent to the final order requires the consenting natural parent to sign a formal agreement (Form 10).

Section 14(1) of the 1952 Act deals with various procedural aspects relating to the giving of a valid consent but primarily provides that an adoption order cannot be made without the consent of the child's mother or guardian, which may include the natural father, or any other person having care or control over the child immediately before it is placed for adoption. Importantly however, s.14(2) provides that no consent is required where the party whose consent is sought either cannot be found or is incapable, by reason of mental infirmity, of giving such consent. In respect of the form of the consent, if it is to be regarded as validly given, it must be in writing (s.14(5)). A consent will not be valid unless the child has attained six weeks of age (s.15(1) as amended). The 1952 Act placed great emphasis on the knowledge of consenting parties regarding their understanding of the nature and effect of both the consent and the ultimate adoption order and provided that the Adoption Board must satisfy itself that such an understanding exists. Section 14(6) represents a further protective measure towards the consenting party, insofar as it permits her to withdraw consent at any time before the making of the adoption order.

Full, free and informed consent

It was stated in *G v An Bord Uchtála* [1980] I.R. 52 that as a general rule an adoption can only proceed with the full, free and informed consent of all the parties whose consent is required under the legislation. This requirement also has a Constitutional basis as to give a child up for adoption involves the waiver by the mother of her personal right to the care and custody of her child, a right guaranteed under Art.40.3.1 of the Constitution. It is well established that the consent given must be meaningful; Walsh J. in *G v An Bord Uchtála* [1980] I.R. 52 re-affirms that the consent "must be such as to amount to a fully-informed, free and willing surrender or an abandonment of these rights". Thus the consequences of both the placement and the final adoption order must be made clear as much as is possible. In *EF and FF v An Bord Uchtála and SD*, unreported, Supreme Court, Keane J., July 17, 1996 the Supreme Court confirmed the s.3(1) order dispensing with the mothers consent to the final adoption order as it was satisfied that "the consequences of a Section 3 order were fully explained to the mother and, most importantly understood by her." Keane J. called for the use of blunt and uncompromising language when explaining the effect of the placement and adoption order to the mother. In addition she must be made aware of her right to withdraw her consent at any time prior to the making of the final order, as confirmed by O'Higgins J. in *M v An Bord Uchtála* [1977] I.R. 287 (the *McL* case). Although it is clearly necessary to explain to the mother the extent of her rights, it was confirmed in *O'C v The Sacred Heart Adoption Society* [1996] I.L.R.M. 297 that it is not necessary to explain the legal source of such rights. Parental pressure or even the perception of parental disapproval may, for instance, render the consent invalid. In *G v An Bord Uchtála*, Walsh J. emphasised that a consent which was granted in circumstances of fear, stress or anxiety, or was dictated by poverty or other deprivations cannot constitute a valid consent. This broad definition of what might vitiate a parental consent was queried subsequently by McWilliam J. in *McF v G and G* [1983] I.L.R.M. 228 when he highlighted the almost unavoidable existence of stress and anxiety in circumstances where a woman is pregnant outside of wedlock. In his view "if absolute rules as to fear, stress, anxiety or poverty were to be applied there could hardly be a case in which one or other would be present so that it could be argued that a consent was not valid" (at 232).

   In *NB and TB v An Bord Uchtála*, unreported, High Court, February 18, 1983, it was held that the mere fact that the mother may not have fully absorbed all the advice and information given to her by a social worker prior to agreeing to place her child for adoption did not, by itself, invalidate an agreement to place where it was clear that at the time of the agreement, the mother wanted her child to be adopted, that the consequences of placing her child for adoption were fully explained to her and at the time of the explanation, the mother understood those consequences. However the opposite view was taken by Laffoy J. in the jointly listed matters of *DG and MG v An Bord Uchtála* and *CG v Pasley and PACT and DG and MG*, unreported, High Court, May 23, 1996. The prospective adoptive parents sought to dispense with the consent of the mother, CG, who had, late in the adoption process sought to secure the return of her child. The central issue for consideration by the court was whether there existed a valid agreement to place the child for adoption. Before considering the evidence of the relevant social worker and the natural mother, Laffoy J. set out the requirements for a mother's consent to the placement of her child for adoption to be fully informed. She state that for a mother to be fully informed, she:

"… must be aware of:–
   (i)   the nature of her rights in relation to the child but without their categorisation as constitutional or legal rights,
  (ii)   the two-stage nature of the adoption process,
 (iii)   the effect of the making of an adoption order on her rights, and
  (iv)   the effect of Section 3 of the Adoption Act 1974 and, in particular, the possibility that, if she gives an initial consent to the placement, this Court may override the requirement of a final consent."

Laffoy J. was of the view that the true test is whether the decision reached by the natural mother "reflects her will or the will of somebody else". She regarded the test as subjective to the capacities and understanding of the mother, which can only be assessed and ascertained from the mother's evidence. Ultimately, the court concluded that the mother did not and could not make a free decision, rather she "subordinated her own will to that of her parents, because of fear, which was a product of her upbringing, stress, anxiety, lack of maturity and deprivation of emotional support." Consequently the agreement to place the child was not valid and the plaintiff's application for a s.3 order dispensing with the consent of the mother was refused.

In DG an infant: OG v An Bord Uchtála [1991] 1 I.R. 491 the central issue for consideration by the court was whether the young mother of the boy placed in the care of the proposed adoptive parents has given full, free and informed consent. It was argued on behalf of the natural mother that she had not been fully and correctly informed of the effects of placing the child for adoption and thus her consent was not validly given. Although Lavan J. refused to make a s.3(1) order in favour of the prospective adoptive parents and granted custody to the natural mother, ultimately the Supreme Court ordered a retrial of the evidence to decide the issue of whether the natural mother had given full, free and informed consent to the adoption process. Whilst the matter was settled between the parties, the case is instructive given the statement of Finlay C.J. regarding the correct approach to be adopted to ensure that a mother can give an informed consent to the adoption process:

> "… it is of obvious importance to state that a mother agreeing to place her child for adoption could not be said to reach a fully informed decision so to agree, unless at the time she made the agreement she was aware that the right which she undoubtedly has to withdraw the consent or to refuse further to consent to adoption, is subject to the possibility that, upon application by the prospective adopting parents, the court could conclude that it was in the best interests of the child to dispense with the mother's consent, and if following such a decision the board decided that it was appropriate to order the adoption of the child, she (the mother) could lose, forever, the custody of the child." (at 515)

Withdrawal of consent

The manner in which consent was dealt with under the 1952 Act ensured that no child could be adopted without the existence of a validly attained consent. Thus as originally statutorily regulated, adoption was established as a consent or voluntary arrangement, and until the final consent was given and the adoption order made, it was within the rights of the consenting parent or guardian to withdraw or refuse to give consent to the adoption process. The difficulties arising from this absolute protection of the consenting party and their right to withdraw consent, often long after the child has been placed with the prospective adoptive parents, was addressed by s.3 of the Adoption Act 1974 which empowers the court to make the adoption order in the absence of consent. Section 3(1) can be invoked by the prospective adopters where the consent to the adoption order has either been refused by the parent or guardian, or the earlier consent to the placement of a child has been withdrawn. This section has been narrowly construed by the court, given that to make such an order is often to over-ride the wishes of the natural mother or father of the child. The section as worded appears to identify a two-stage process of consent; firstly requiring consent or agreement to the placing of a child for adoption, and secondly a later consent to the making of the final adoption order. The existence of two stages within the adoption process was confirmed by Walsh J. in *G v An Bord Uchtála* [1980] I.R. 52, regarding it as an adoption code involving "two separate and distinct consents". Importantly, he emphasised the lack of finality arising from the consent to place a child for adoption, and that such a consent must be regarded as interim in nature and must not be construed as an abandonment or waiver on the part of the mother of her right to custody.

When a child is placed for adoption with the full, free and informed consent of those persons required, s.14(6) of the 1952 Act allows the consenting party to withdraw the consent at any time before the making of an adoption order. Where the consent is withdrawn at a late stage and the child is already with the adoptive parents, judicial intervention is typically sought. In such circumstances, the court must determine the issues of the custody of the child on the basis of the "best interests of the child" test. Under s.3 of the Adoption Act 1974, the High Court can make an order that the consent is no longer required and in so doing must consider what is in the best interest of the child.

Withdrawal of consent: case law

One of the first cases to consider the powers arising from s.3 was *G v An Bord Uchtála* [1980] I.R. 32. Walsh J. regarded the new provision as "a radical departure" from the pre-existing adoption structure which given its significance falls outside the remit of the Adoption Board and can only be dealt with by the High Court. Ultimately he was of the view that in considering an application under s.3, the court cannot make the order sought unless satisfied that it is in the best interests of the child. In the matter of *J.O'D an infant, the Northern Area Health Board, WH and PH v An Bord Uchtála and P.O'D* [2002] 4 I.R. 252 Herbert J. emphasised the courts role in intervening where appropriate in the adoption process where, notwithstanding the withdrawal of consent by the mother, the court is compelled to dispense with her consent in the best interests of the child. It was held that a withdrawal of consent and a stated desire for communication and meetings with the child should never be sufficient to negate proof of abandonment. To so disregard such evidence of abandonment would, in his view, entirely "set at nought" the object of the Oireachtas in enacting the 1988 Act.

The issues of parental consent, the marriage of natural parents post placement of their child and the consequences of the withdrawal of consent prior to the making of the final order have recently been adjudicated upon by both the High Court and Supreme Court. In *N v Health Service Executive and An Bord Uchtála* [2006] 4 I.R. 374 the court was asked to rule on the custody of a two-year-old girl, known for the purpose of the hearing as Baby Ann, who immediately after her birth in July 2004 was placed with foster parents with a view to adoption. Prior to the making of the final adoption order, less than a year after she had been placed for adoption, the mother withdrew her consent. The natural parents married in January 2006 and thereafter applied to the courts for the return of baby Ann. In the High Court, McMenamin J. considered the provisions of Arts 41 and 42 of the Constitution and noted that there exists a constitutional presumption that the needs of children are best met and their welfare secured within the family. However equally, McMenamin J. in high-lighting the rebuttable nature of this presumption sought to rely upon the statement of Walsh J. in *McGee v Attorney General* [1974] I.R. 284:

> "... that is not to say that the authority of parents is absolute or that they are immune from State intervention in all circumstances when exercising that authority." (at 310)

McMenamin J. accepted the evidence before the court that in removing the child from her proposed adoptive parents there was a high probability of a risk of harm or psychological damage to the child. To rebut the presumption that the interests of a child are best served within the natural family, required evidence of either a failure of parental duty or the existence of the "compelling reasons" to show otherwise. In this regard, an objective test was to be applied to identify a failure of parental duty. In the circumstances, McMenamin J. was satisfied that the presumption had been successfully rebutted under both tests. The decision was over-ruled on appeal to the Supreme Court, where the court unanimously ordered that the child should be returned to the natural parents as the constitutional presumption in their favour had not been rebutted under either test. It was confrimed that the placement for adoption should not be regarded as evidence of a failure of parental duty, nor should it constitute one of the factors leading to a conclusion of abandonment.

Consent of the natural father

The provisions of the 1952 Act did not include the natural father of a child as one of the parties entitled to be consulted or to be heard by the Adoption Board on an application for an adoption order. The position was somewhat improved by s.2 of the Adoption Act 1964 where a child whose status has been legitimated is the subject of an adoption application. Where the parents of a child have married subsequent to the birth of that child and whose birth has not been re-registered, the consent of the father is required in relation to the making of the adoption order. Since then, the Status of Children Act 1987 entitles the natural father to apply to be appointed the guardian of his child, and this greatly strengthens the position of the natural father generally and also within the adoption process as it cannot proceed without the consent of the guardian(s) of the child. In effect, the father, if appointed a guardian, can veto the adoption process. Thus, up to this point, the natural father of a child who was not a legal guardian of that child did not have to be consulted and had no right to be heard nor did he have any rights in respect of giving his consent. However, the Adoption Act 1998 now requires adoption agencies, pursuant to s.4, which inserted Pt 1A into the 1952 Act, to hear the views of the father of a child who is the subject of a proposed adoption order. The right to be consulted extends to the father or the person who believes himself to be the father of the child. The 1998 Act places an onus on the adoption agency to make contact with the father, or where his identity is unknown or undisclosed, the agency if further obliged under s.7F(3) to endeavour to ascertain the identity of the natural father, which might necessitate the counselling of the mother regarding the consequences of such refusal. Thus the natural father of the child must now be contacted irrespective of whether he has guardianship status. In addition, a person who believes he is the father of a child subject to the adoption process, is entitled to be contacted and heard. The pre-placement process may be dispensed with where the agency is unable to contact the father, or declines to do so due to the nature of the relationship between the father and the mother or the circumstances of the conception of the child. Whatever the circumstances, s.4 further empowers the agency to place the child for adoption where the father either (a) indicates that he has no objection to the placement or (b) the adoption agency is unable to or chooses not to consult the father.

In the event of the refusal by the mother to disclose the identity of the father of the child, the agency is statutorily obliged to provide her with counselling to emphasise the importance of this information. Where the mother continues to refuse to disclose his identity, the agency must submit to the Adoption Board, a report on the nature of the counselling made available to her. If satisfied, the Board may then authorise the adoption notwithstanding the failure to consult the father (s.19A inserted by s.6). Where the father has been contacted and has refused to grant consent, the matter is adjourned for at least 21 days to allow the father to issue guardianship proceedings and the child may not be placed for adoption until these proceedings are completed (s.7E(3)(1)). Where the father does not take the matter further during those 21 days, the adoption can proceed. Where the unmarried father of the child has guardianship status his consent is required for the adoption to proceed and ultimately his unwillingness to consent to the adoption would empower him to veto the adoption.

The rights of the unmarried father of a child being placed for adoption were addressed by various courts in the resolution of the Keegan case. In *K v W* [1990] 2 I.R. 437 the unmarried father of a child placed for adoption sought to challenge the adoption process. The case concerned a child born to unmarried parents, although the pregnancy was planned. However after the birth of the child, the parties split up and the mother placed the child for adoption, without the consent or the knowledge of the natural father. Although he had no right to be consulted under the terms of the 1952 Act, nor was his consent required at that time he did apply for guardianship. On the facts, and because at that point the child had been with the adoptive parents for 15 months, it was held that the child's best interests were served with leaving her with the adoptive parents. The court recognised that the application of the father for guardianship status was closely linked to his intention to oppose the adoption process and that in essence the question to be determined before the father could be appointed guardian, was whether he should also be granted custody. Barron J. admitted his willingness to appoint the applicant father as a guardian of the child, but declared himself unable to do so in the circumstances as the consequential disruption to the child's current living arrangements would not have been in her best interests. Similarly in *WO'R v EH and An Bord Uchtála* [1996] 2 I.R. 248 the Supreme Court confirmed that on hearing an application by a natural father to be appointed guardian, it is proper for the court to take into account a specific pending application for adoption of the children, to include the taking into account of the natural father's intention to oppose the adoption application. In the earlier case, K., otherwise Keegan applied to the European Court of Human Rights on the basis that his rights under Arts 6 and 8 had been violated. The court found in his favour, stating that he did have family ties with the child, his right to a fair hearing had been denied, he had had no chance to challenge the placement decision and it was wrong that he had no standing in the adoption proceedings generally. As a result of this decision adoption agencies changed their practices to involve the father, where he could be identified and contacted.

9. STATE INTERVENTION IN THE FAMILY

Introduction

Given the position of the family under Art.41.1 of the Constitution as an institution that possesses "inalienable and imprescriptible rights, antecedent and superior to all positive law", the State has a very limited right to intervene in the autonomy of the family. The right of the state to interfere with the care and upbringing of a child has depended for the most part on the development by the courts of independent constitutional rights of the child which in extreme circumstances can only be vindicated when removed from the home. Whilst the family as a unit is protected by Arts 41 and 43, Art.42.5 highlights parental obligations in respect of their children. In exceptional cases where parents have failed in their duty towards their children it is open to the State to intervene with a view to defending the welfare of the children. In conjunction with this, legislation has been enacted to place a positive onus on the State to intervene where necessary. Ultimately it is for the parents to have responsibility and care for the children, with the State intervening in the event of the child being in a position of danger.

As a starting point, the Constitution expressly authorises state intervention in the family where circumstances so require. Article 42.5 authorises the State to intervene on behalf of children where parents have failed for physical or moral reasons in their duty towards their children. The inclusion of such a provision reflects the drafters' desire to provide the State with a residual right of intervention in extreme circumstances of physical or moral failure on the part of the parents of a child. In light of the elevated status of the family in the Constitution and its position being "superior to all positive law", failure to include this provision would most likely have prevented, or certainly made it very difficult for the state to intervene where necessary. The issue has received judicial attention in a number of cases. The right of the State to interfere with the autonomy of the family was clearly stated by Geoghegan J. in *FN (a minor) v Minister for Education and others*, unreported, High Court, March 24, 1995 which considered an application for a care order under the Child Care Act 1991 ("the 1991 Act"), involving a child with a disorder. He confirmed the constitutional obligation on the state under Art.42.5 to cater for the needs of a child with special needs where such care cannot be provided by the parents or guardians. The right of the State to interfere with the autonomy of the family was clearly stated by Geoghegan J. in *FN (a minor) v Minister for Education*, unreported, High Court, March 24, 2005 which considered an application for a care order under the 1991 Act, involving a child with a disorder. He spoke of the state's constitutional obligations towards the applicant child to make suitable arrangements for that child. Kelly J. in *O'B v Minister for Justice, Minister for Health and others* [1999] 1 I.R. 29, had previously stated that the court was obliged to ensure that those expectations are realised.

Transfer of powers and responsibilities to the Health Services Executive

The 1991 Act accords the statutory powers and responsibilities to the Health Boards, defined by s.2 of the 1991 Act as "a health board established under the Health Act 1970". However s.6 of the Health Act 2004 established the body to be known as the Health Services Executive (HSE) and s.58 of the 2004 Act provided for the dissolution of the existing Health Boards, with the consequential transfer of powers and responsibilities of the Health Boards to the HSE.

Child Care Act 1991

The main purpose of the 1991 Act, as enacted, is to provide a means by which the welfare and protection of children can be safeguarded. In extreme circumstances, the 1991 Act authorises State interference whereby a child can be removed from the care, custody and authority of his parents and delivered into the care of the State. The emphasis in the Act is on the protection of children in a family environment and it is only when this approach has failed that the more interventionist aspects of the legislation will be employed. In this regard, s.3(2)(c) requires the HSE to have regard to the principle that it is generally in the best interests of the child to be brought up in his own family. When making any order under the 1991 Act, the court, having regard to the rights and duties of parents, whether under the Constitution or otherwise, is obliged under s.24 to:

(a) regard the welfare of the child as the first and paramount consideration, and

(b) in so far as is practicable, give due consideration, having regard to his age and understanding, to the wishes of the child.

Circumstances requiring State intervention in the family

The nature of the State intervention and provision of care arises from both Constitutional and statutory provisions and can loosely be divided into:

- Voluntary care,
- Care in emergencies,
- Care necessitating supervisory involvement by the HSE without removing the child from the family environment, and
- Care requiring the removal of the child from the custody of a parent or parents.

Voluntary care

Section 4 obliges the State to intervene and take the child into care where it appears that he requires care and protection that he would not otherwise receive if not taken into care. The child can be removed from the home under this section for so long as his welfare requires it, having regard to the wishes of his parents. However this section cannot be relied upon by the HSE unless the parents have consented to the removal. Where a parent wishes to resume care, the HSE has no authority under s.4, or in light of the earlier consent, to maintain the child in its care. The issue of parental consent arose in the High Court case of *DO'H v HSE and TH* [2007] I.E.H.C. 175 where the non-married father with guardianship status sought a declaration from the court that the children's placement in foster care was invalid for want of his consent. His claim to be entitled to object to their foster care on the basis of s.4(2) of the 1991 Act which requires the HSE, when taking a child into voluntary care, to do so with the consent of the "parent having custody of him". As guardian of the children, the applicant claimed to come within this category of persons. In this regard Abbott J. was very sympathetic to the position of the non-married guardian father and noted in the circumstances before the court, that the consent of both parents was required.

Protection of children in emergencies

Part III of the 1991 Act is headed "Protection of Children in Emergencies" and provides the statutory basis for protecting children in emergency situations. It permits the intervention in cases of emergency by the members of the Garda Síochána and the HSE, with the assistance of the courts. In extreme instances, s.12 empowers members of the Garda

Síochána to take a child into safety where there are reasonable grounds for believing there is an immediate and serious risk to the health or welfare of the child and it would be insufficient to await the making of an emergency care order.

Section 13 sets out the court route in instances of emergency care and provides for the placement of a child in the care of the HSE for a period of eight or less days where:

(a) there is an immediate and serious risk to the health or welfare of the child which necessitates him being placed in the care of the HSE; or

(b) there is likely to be such a risk if the child is removed from the place where he is for the time being.

Such an application can, if necessitated by circumstances, be made on an ex parte basis. The HSE is obliged under s.14 to notify the parents or person in loco parentis that the child has been placed in care.

Care proceedings (non-emergency)

Where the HSE is of the view that a child in its area is in need of care or protection which he is unlikely to receive unless an appropriate order is made by the court, and the immediate removal of the child is not necessitated, s.16 requires the HSE to make an application to the court for a care order or a supervision order, as appropriate.

Interim care order

Section 17 of the 1991 Act governs the application for and granting of an interim care order, the aim of which is to protect the child in the short term. An interim care order can last for up to eight days and will be made where the court is satisfied that:

(a) the child has been or is being assaulted, ill-treated, neglected or sexually abused; or

(b) the child's health, development or welfare has been or is being avoidably impaired or neglected; or

(c) the child's health, development or welfare is likely to be avoidably impaired or neglected.

Supervision order

Section 19 provides a less interventionist approach and authorises the HSE to periodically visit the child at home, on such occasions as the HSE deems necessary to advise the parents regarding the care of the child and/or to satisfy itself as to the welfare of the child. A court can make such a supervision order where it is satisfied that there are reasonable grounds for believing that:

(a) the child has been or is being assaulted, ill-treated, neglected or sexually abused; or

(b) the child's health, development or welfare has been or is being avoidably impaired or neglected; or

(c) the child's health, development or welfare is likely to be avoidably impaired or neglected,

and it is desirable that the child be visited periodically by or on behalf of the health board. The supervision order permits ongoing supervision and involvement on the part of the HSE but remains less intrusive than a care order. Dissatisfied parents can, under s.19(3), apply to the court for directions in relation to the nature of the visits. The HSE can equally seek the assistance of the court where necessary; the court can give directions under s.19(4) on application by the HSE, requiring the parents to bring the child to a medical or psychiatric examination, treatment or assessment.

Care order

The effect of the care order is to commit the child in need of care or protection to the care of the HSE for so long as he remains a child or for a shorter period of time. The HSE is authorised to make such an order where it is satisfied that:

(a) the child has been or is being assaulted, ill-treated, neglected or sexually abused; or

(b) the child's health, development or welfare has been or is being avoidably impaired or neglected; or

(c) the child's health, development or welfare is likely to be avoidably impaired or neglected,

and that the child requires care and protection, which he is unlikely to receive unless the order is made. The court can extend the period of time for which the order applies, either on its own motion or on the application of another person, if it satisfied that the grounds for the making of the order continue to exist.

Role of the Health Services Executive

Section 3(1) of the 1991 Act requires the HSE to promote the welfare of children who are not receiving adequate care and protection. In performing this function, the HSE shall, pursuant to s.3(2):

(a) take such steps as it considers requisite to identify children who are not receiving adequate care and protection and co-ordinate information from all relevant sources relating to children in its area;

(b) having regard to the rights and duties of parents, whether under the Constitution or otherwise—

    (i) regard the welfare of the child as the first and paramount consideration, and

    (ii) in so far as is practicable, give due consideration, having regard to his age and understanding, to the wishes of the child; and

(c) have regard to the principle that it is generally in the best interests of a child to be brought up in his own family.

The case of *Eastern Health Board v E, A and A* [2000] 1 I.R. 430 concerned a complaint made by the Eastern Health Board that Baby A was being unlawfully detained by the respondents, contrary to a previous order of the court. The history behind the making of an order related to the attempt by the mother of the child to agree a private adoption of her baby by the first and second-named respondents. The Health Board was notified of the situation because of a similar attempt by the first and second-named respondents to privately adopt another baby, Baby B. Although for the most part the judgment of Laffoy J. concerned the relevant adoption laws, the court also considered the role of the Health Board in preventing private adoptions. In her view, the decision by Baby A's mother to place her in the custody of strangers was a decision which seriously compromised the welfare of Baby A and it was a decision that the Health Board, in fulfilment of its functions under the 1991 Act was bound to seek to address.

Role of the court

The extent of the involvement of the court in attaching conditions to orders made under the 1991 Act was considered by the District Court and later reviewed by the High Court in *Eastern Health Board v Judge JP McDonnell* [1999] I.R. 174. McDonnell J. of the District Court had made care orders under the 1991 Act in respect of two children, placing them in the care of the Eastern Health Board. However in making such orders McDonnell J. was critical of the care provided for the children by the Health Board to date, and ordered that there should be no further changes in the appointed foster parents or social worker without leave of the court. The Health Board argued that the court did not have jurisdiction beyond the making of the care order and that it was the duty and responsibility of the Health Board to draw up the care plan for the children. In the High Court, McCracken J. relied upon s.47 of the 1991 Act which gives the District Court a wide jurisdiction in child care cases, which is not limited to cases where proceedings are before the court. Section 47 provides that where a child is in the care of a health board, the District Court may, of its own motion or on the application of any person, give such directions and make such order on any question affecting the welfare of the child as it thinks proper and may vary or discharge any such direction or order. McCracken J. regarded this section as entitling the District Court, where necessary, to impose directions in relation to children in the care of the health board as it retains ultimate responsibility for such children under the 1991 Act.

Kelly J. in the High Court challenged the approach of the executive in his judgment in *TD (a minor) v Minister for Education, Ireland, A.G., Eastern Health Board and Minister for Health and Children*, unreported, High Court, February 25, 2000. The applicant claimed that the State had failed to fulfil its Constitutional obligations to provide for the accommodation needs of children with particular problems. He was one of a group of disadvantaged children in need of accommodation and treatment in high support units. As the respondents had formulated a policy to deal with the general problem of children with special needs, the proceedings were adjourned before the High Court to allow for the implementation of this policy. When the respondents failed to implement this policy in a timely manner, the applicant and others sought an injunction directing the respondents to provide facilities in accordance with the stated policy. In the High Court, Kelly J. was highly critical of the approach of the executive to date and in particular the failure on the part of the executive to meet these obligations. In this regard, Kelly J. directed the executive to meet the needs of the applicant. However, the Supreme Court overturned his ruling, stating that the court has no right to make mandatory orders against two Ministers of the executive; such orders being inconsistent with the distribution of powers under the separation of powers doctrine ([2001] 4 I.R. 259). However Keane J. did acknowledge that to the extent that it might exist, the right to be placed and maintained in secure residential accommodation must be one of the unenumerated personal rights guaranteed under Art.40.3.1 and where children have behavioural problems, the needs normally met by parents must be upheld by the State.

Parental autonomy v State intervention

Where an application for state intervention in the family is before the court, the decision to authorise or order such intervention can only be made following an assessment of the circumstances in which the child or children are living. The court must satisfy itself pursuant to the tests set out in the 1991 Act that HSE intervention and/or removal of the child is so necessary as to over-ride the constitutional protection and autonomy of the family unit. The importance placed on parental and familial autonomy in the Constitution is mirrored in the 1991 Act. Certain fundamental principles and presumptions are outlined in the Act to guide the approach of the HSE and the decision-making process of the courts. As set out above, when fulfilling its basic functions under s.3 of the 1991 Act, the HSE is obliged to "have regard to the principle that it is generally in the best interests of a child to be brought up in his own family" (s.3(2)(c)).

Case law

In *A and B v Eastern Health Board* [1998] 1 I.R. 464 the High Court reviewed the interim care order made by the District Court under s.17 of the 1991 Act in respect of a 13-year-old girl. The central issue for consideration concerned the directions given by the court under s.17(4) to permit the Health Board to take the steps necessary to arrange for the termination of the child's pregnancy. The power of the court to make this order was challenged by the parents, A and B. One of the grounds of challenge set out by the parents was that the court had failed to have proper regard to their rights and duties as required by s.24 of the 1991 Act. The District Court judge in making her decision disregarded the wishes of the parents who were opposed to the abortion. On consideration of the evidence, Geoghegan J. also refused the relief sought by the natural parents, stating that full regard had been given to their rights and duties.

The issue of balancing the needs of the child with the autonomy of the parents was the central issue in *North Western Health Board v HW and CW* [2001] 3 I.R. 622. The original application for state intervention was brought by the North Western Health Board, which sought a court order to carry out a standard screening test on the respondents' child to detect relatively common conditions, treatable if discovered early. The respondent parents were members of the Jehovah's Witness faith and objected to such a test. The Health Board sought declarations authorising the test on the basis that it was in the best interests of the child. In the High Court, McCracken J. considered the extent to which state intervention can be authorised where there is a conflict between the wishes of the parents and the best medical advice. He was of the view that in extreme cases, decisions of parents that put children into risk situations would justify state intervention. In this regard, he noted that the Constitution permits the State to intervene in exceptional cases where the parents fail in their duty towards their child, as legislatively provided for in the 1991 Act. However, although McCracken J. regarded the carrying out of the screening test as in the best interests of the child, he concluded that to allow the State to intervene in every case where professional opinion differed from the parents' opinion would be at variance with the spirit and words of the Constitution. Thus the order was refused, the impugned decision, made by "caring and conscientious parents" was not an exceptional case, despite general medical opinion that they were wrong.

On appeal by the North Western Health Board, the majority of the five-judge Supreme Court confirmed the decision of McCracken J. to refuse the order, with Keane C.J. dissenting. Denham J. noted the constitutional presumption that the welfare of the child is to be found within the family, thus the decision required a weighing and balancing of constitutional principles. To permit intervention in the family would require the existence of exceptional circumstances which could only be determined on the facts of each case, but would include an immediate threat to the health or life of the child. Denham J. rejected the Health Board's application, as to compel the test would establish a very low threshold for court intervention in future cases in relation to children. Whilst she acknowledged that the welfare of the child is the paramount consideration, this must be considered with due regard to the fact that it is usually in the best interests of the child to be brought up in his own family. This view was supported by Murphy, Murray and Hardiman JJ. Murphy J. regarded state intervention as potentially damaging to the long term interests of the child given the erosion of the interest and dedication of the parents in the performance of their duties. In his view, State intervention should only arise where either:

"... the general conduct or circumstances of the parents is such as to constitute a virtual abdication of their responsibilities or alternatively the disastrous consequences of a particular parental decision are so immediate and inevitable as to demand intervention and perhaps call into question either the basic competence or devotion of the parents". (para.209)

However Murray J. emphasised that parental authority is not absolute, quoting Walsh J. in *McGee v Attorney General* [1974] I.R. 284 that "... the State is the guardian of the common good ...". He emphasised that whilst it is well established that the family as a moral institution enjoys certain liberties under the Constitution which protect it from undue interference by the State, the State may intervene in exceptional circumstances in the interest of the common good or where the parents have failed for physical or moral reasons in their duty towards their children. In his dissenting judgment, quoting Walsh J. the Supreme Court in *G v An Bord Uchtála* [1980] I.R. 32, Keane C.J. noted that: "... One of the duties of a parent or parents, be they married or not, is to provide as best the parent or parents can, the welfare of the child and to ward off dangers to the health", and in his view the parents had failed to protect and vindicate the constitutional right of the child to be guarded against unnecessary and avoidable dangers to his health and welfare, which in his view was the responsibility of the court. The majority decision in this case reflects the high thresholds applied by the court in determining circumstances appropriate for state intervention in the family.

Scope of the powers of the Health Services Executive

Less than typical circumstances arose in *Western Health Board v KM*, unreported, High Court, McGuinness J., December 21, 2001 involving the respondent's child TK, who was in the care of the Western Health Board. The Health Board sought a direction confirming its authority to place the child with a relative in the United Kingdom which gave rise to a District Court consultative case stated to the High Court requesting clarification of the following:

1. Whether the health board has a power of placement with relatives outside the state under s.36 of the 1991 Act?
2. Whether the court has a power of placement with relatives outside the state under s.47 of the 1991 Act?
3. If yes under either section of the 1991 Act, can the period of placement be limited?

The judgment of the High Court, delivered by Finnegan J. rejected the suggestion that the Health Board has a power of placement outside this jurisdiction under s.36 of the 1991 Act. Finnegan J. highlighted the duty of the HSE to "maintain control and supervision" over any child that is in its care. Thus whilst s.18(3)(b)(iii) allows the HSE to consent to the issue of a passport for the child, this is to enable him/her to "travel abroad for a limited period" and was not intended to authorise foster care outside the jurisdiction. Further, to send the child abroad, even for foster care, would represent "an abandonment by a health board of the control which a care order vests in it". However a far less restrictive approach was taken to s.47 which empowers the court, of its own motion or on application by any person, to "give such directions and make such order on any question affecting the welfare of the child as it thinks proper". Thus the provision was deemed by Finnegan J. to permit the court "to do whatever it deems appropriate to achieve the policy of the Act as a whole" which included directing the placement of a child with relatives outside the State, where appropriate. In addition, as there is no limitation on the District Court's power to act under s.47 of the 1991 Act, it could direct the placement to be with or without a time limit. This decision was later affirmed by the Supreme Court, McGuinness J. viewing the 1991 Act as a remedial social statute that should be approached in a purposive and liberal manner.

INDEX